Our Home

Our Home

Where Your Story Begins

CM Mary

OUR HOME
WHERE YOUR STORY BEGINS

iUniverse books may be ordered through booksellers or by contacting:

*iUniverse LLC
1663 Liberty Drive
Bloomington, IN 47403
www.iuniverse.com
1-800-Authors (1-800-288-4677)*

*Because of the dynamic nature of the Internet, any web
addresses or links contained in this book may have changed
since publication and may no longer be valid. The views
expressed in this work are solely those of the author and do
not necessarily reflect the views of the publisher, and the
publisher hereby disclaims any responsibility for them.*

*Any people depicted in stock imagery provided by Thinkstock are
models, and such images are being used for illustrative purposes only.
Certain stock imagery © Thinkstock.*

*ISBN: 978-1-4917-3489-6 (sc)
ISBN: 978-1-4917-3490-2 (e)*

Library of Congress Control Number: 2014909479

Printed in the United States of America.

iUniverse rev. date: 06/19/2014

Contents

For Mom and Dad

The greatest wealth is health.
Virgil (17-90 BC)

Foreword

CM Mary loves to write. She has been keeping journals for more than fifteen years. She has written three books of personal stories for her two children. They are stories about them growing up in Milladore, WI. She has always said, "Home is where everyone's story begins." I hope you enjoy this book which are stories about her parents and siblings.

Valerie Milz
Daughter of CM Mary

Preface

Let me introduce the eight main characters that are in the pages of this book.

Ralph Frank (Pat) Schmitt is our Dad and was born November 24th, 1925. He married our Mom, Mary Margaret Eder on September 14, 1946. She was born on May 5th, 1927. They began their married life in Illinois but moved to Wisconsin in 1968. Only four of the six of us moved with them because two of us were going to Northern Illinois University at the time of the move. The six of us are:

Constance Mary (Schmitt) Milz born June 7, 1948 aka Connie

Patricia Lee (Schmitt) Sauber born January 5, 1950 aka Pat or Patty

Pamela Ann (Schmitt) Meyer born February 5, 1953 aka Pam

Ralph Frank Schmitt JR. born February 18, 1956 aka JR

Nancy Josephine (Schmitt) (Milz) Locknane born September 9, 1957 aka Nance

CM Mary

Albert James Schmitt born April 18, 1962 aka Al and more

This is my first attempt to write a book that I can have published for Dad to make available for his children, grandchildren, and great-grandchildren. For a few years I have written for a local newspaper using the pen name CM Mary. Writing short articles seems to be easier than an entire book but I have tried to break this task down into a series of short stories. I am the first born in this family, which does make me the oldest. There have been times when I wanted, and did, list my birth year as 1958. It isn't like I regret growing old because I know a few people that have been denied that privilege. This book puts an end to that because once it is in print, the truth will be there for everyone to see. In all honesty, I don't think I was really fooling many people.

The only regret I have is that I didn't write this book while my Mother was alive. We found lots of interesting things in our Mother's belongings after her death. One thing Mom always said was that you should write on the back of your pictures. She followed her advice, in many cases, by writing on the back of most of her pictures. We did find some that must have been from her high school days that we can't identify. I decided I would make up a story using those pictures. They are not part of this project; there is no fiction here. Family folklore or urban legend maybe, but this is a work of non-fiction.

1/Home is where our story begins

My parents are attending a high school dance. Mom graduated from high school in 1945 so this picture was around that time. It looks like they were having fun.

The best thing a Father can do for his children, is love their mother. Our Dad did just that for 61 years before our Mother's death in 2008. They raised six of us during their life together creating a home for us where we knew we were loved and could feel safe. Our stories or "family folklore" come from the years we spent together. The word "folklore" can be described as oral history, popular beliefs, or tall tales; just to name a few ways to define that word. In this book I plan to record our family folklore along with the help of Dad, my sisters and brothers. They will all be introduced further as this story progresses. To get everyone's input I asked them to think about their favorite family stories. Dad came up with a favorite story for each of his children as well as his sisters and brothers. The audacity of our little sister Pam became apparent with Dad's story about her. That tale is to follow in Pam's chapter.

One family tale that has taken on the distinction of folklore is the screen door event. I remember hearing this story and I think it was Dad's mother who told me about the broken screen door on the farm. When Dad was just a little guy he wanted to sleep outside on a very warm summer night. When I was told about this story I pictured Dad as an 8-year old. He got a blanket and pillow and settled under a tree in the back lawn for a good night's sleep. All was fine until two cats started to quarrel, which can create lots of noise; and in the house he ran going through the screen door because it had been locked by mistake. Dad can't verify the story but he said it could have happened.

Dad can verify the honeymoon story because he wrote about it in his memoir. He and mom were married on September 14, 1946 at St Mary's in Maple Park, Illinois. Their wedding dance was in the town hall where years later we had our 4-H meetings. Dad was working for his father on the farm at the time and September is harvest time, which doesn't change even for a wedding. Dad said they went to Maywood, Illinois for the weekend and came home to finish filling the silo. It wasn't until a month later that they went on an official honeymoon heading for Niagara Falls. They stayed with his sister, Kay in Indianapolis, Indiana over night. Kay's family was moving to another home at the time so Mom and Dad helped them with the move. The next day they started out again for Niagara Falls making it as far as Sandusky, Ohio when Dad's stomach pain got so bad they had to go to an emergency room. His appendix was inflamed and had to be removed. Dad needed to stay in the hospital for a week. He explained that his mother came to stay with Mom at the time but Dad isn't sure how Grandma got to Ohio because she never learned to drive. They never made it to Niagara Falls until years later after a few of us were born. It is said that good things come to those who wait.

There were many family pictures of the eight of us taken when we were young and everyone was still living at home. Our aunt, Diane commented on the fact that there were so many formal pictures of us. That was our Mom: dress everybody up in his or her Sunday best and hire somebody with a camera.

After her death, when we went through all Mom's pictures I took about 30 of them to make an album for each of her children. I only made 5 copies of each and didn't put the originals in just one album but spread them out so each of us had a few of those originals. I recorded the comments from the back of the pictures before it was placed in the albums.

This made a wonderful Christmas gift for my siblings the December after Mom died.

About 20 years ago I was updating one of my computers and asked my parents if they wanted to use my old one. Mom didn't want anything to do with it but Dad was willing to try. He latched on to searching the internet and I taught him to e-mail. He never learned to type but he can find his way around a keyboard. His current computer is bigger than mine and I am still on dial-up while he has moved on to wireless. He even will "Skpe" with Patty in Michigan. We get at least one message a day from Dad because he knows how to forward something that he has received. The following is one of the messages he sent us. This one is a tearjerker, so be careful.

"A young and successful executive was traveling down a neighborhood street, going a bit too fast in his new Jaguar. He was watching for kids darting out from between parked cars and slowed down when he thought he saw something. As his car passed, no children appeared. Instead, a brick smashed into the Jag's side door! He slammed on the brakes and backed the Jag back to the spot where the brick had been thrown. The angry driver then jumped out of the car, grabbed the nearest kid and pushed him up against the car shouting. "What was that all about and who are you? Just what the heck are you doing? That's a new car and that brick you threw is going to cost a lot of money. Why did you do it?' The young boy was apologetic. "Please, mister . . . please, I'm sorry but I didn't know what else to do," He pleaded. "I threw the brick because no one else would stop." With tears running down his face and off his chin, the youth pointed to a spot just around a parked car. "It's my brother," he said "he rolled off the curb and fell out of his wheelchair and I can't lift him up." Now sobbing, the boy asked the stunned executive, "Would you please help me get him back into his wheelchair? He's hurt and he's too heavy for me." Moved beyond words, the driver tried to swallow the rapidly swelling lump in his throat. He hurriedly lifted the handicapped boy back into the wheelchair, then took out a linen handkerchief and dabbed at the fresh scrapes and cuts. A quick look told him everything was going to be okay. 'Thank you and God bless you," the grateful child told the stranger. Too shook up for words, the man simply watched the boy push his wheelchair-bound brother down the sidewalk toward their home. It was a long, slow walk back to the Jaguar. The damage was very noticeable, but the driver never bothered to repair the dented side door. He kept the dent there to remind him of this message: "Don't go through life so fast that someone has to throw a brick at you to get your attention." God whispers in our souls and speaks to our hearts, sometimes when we don't have time to listen, He has to throw a brick at us. It's our choice to listen or not pay any attention."

The reason I used this story is because it reminds me of something my Dad would say when we were young. When you asked Dad if he had a minute to help you his reply was, "I've got more time than money." Isn't that a nice thought? When I was working and raising my two children there were times when I believed it was just the opposite for me. But keep in mind we all have the same 24 hours in a day. Moving on, I have one question; who starts these stories and sends them out so people can forward them to their family and friends? Are there people sitting at computers who have a job that requires them to dream this stuff up and put it on the web? Or is it just a hobby for someone who doesn't work at a computer all day for their regular job? Those questions will not be answered here but I had to ask. Dad doesn't stop at thought provoking stories; he loves to send jokes and political messages. There is no end to him because he is retired and enjoying life.

Another e-story Dad selected and sent or forwarded to us was "statements you don't hear anymore." As I was recording our family history the following statements did make me stop and think about the past. Read them and see if it does the same for you. If not, then you are too young to be in my generation and I wonder what will be written 20 to 30 years from now to make you stop and think about your history? I selected only ten of the twenty-five that was in the original forwarded e-mail.

Be sure to refill those ice trays.
Wash your feet before you go to bed, you've been playing outside all day barefooted.
Take that empty bottle to the store with you so you won't have to pay a deposit on another one.
Quit jumping on the floor! I have a cake in the oven and it will fall if you don't quit!
There's a dollar in my purse, get 5 gallons of gas when you go to town.
You can walk to the store; it won't hurt you to get some exercise.
Don't sit so close to the TV you're going to go blind!
No! I don't have 10 cents for you to go to the show.
If you get a spanking in school and I find out about it, you'll get another one when you get home.
Hurry up and finish drying the dishes so we can go catch some lightning bugs and put them in a jar.

While all of those statements bring back a memory, my favorite was about getting in trouble at school and then getting in trouble again when you arrived home. Of course, parents found out if you were in trouble because there were siblings, cousins, or neighbors to tell on you.

Mary Margaret (Eder) Schmitt; my mother, died March 5, 2008, she was just two months from her 81st birthday. Her life's work is reflected in her six children. Before I explain where we are in life let me reflect on how we were cared for as children. The bee story comes to mind. One summer day when I was twelve and my younger brother, Ralph was four; we were playing outside. A little background information for this story; I am the oldest and terrified of bees. None of us liked bees but I was truly terrified which is a simple fact. Our playing was interrupted by two bees, which I saw on top of my brother's head as he was crying and screaming. He was also running toward me on his way to the house and Mom. I took off away from him also headed for the safety of the house as Mom came out the back door toward him. From my vantage point, which was now inside the house, I saw my mother grab the bees off Ralph's head. She squished them in her hand and threw them to the ground. Not yet finished with the dead bees, she smashed them with her feet. No one messed with Mary Margaret's kids. We always felt safe and loved. Mom worked hard to stay ahead of the laundry for six children. We had clean nicely pressed clothes whenever we headed off to school or church. More than once Mom would be up late on a Sunday night getting our gym clothes ready for Monday morning. We were supposed to get that stuff into the laundry on Friday night but I seldom did. When I started my homework Sunday evening was when the dirty gym clothes were discovered. Those gym suits were freshly pressed and folded on our books on Monday morning. Mom was also very proud of all six of us. Once when she was talking with Aunt Clara, I overheard Mom say that all her children received A's or B's in school. Mom explained that the nuns at the Catholic grade school we attended expected everyone to work hard and learn. She never tired of relating the accomplishments of her children no matter if the goal attained was large or small. The six of us did all graduate from high school with two of us going on to higher education. So where are those six children now? Four of us live and work in Wisconsin close to our parent's home. There are two sisters that have moved to Michigan and Minnesota. We get together several times a year: Christmas, family reunion, or whenever the Michigan and Minnesota sisters can get to Wisconsin. While we don't agree on everything in our lives we are able to get together and enjoy each other's company for a day or two. This is not true of all families and we are blessed because of our parents and their skill at raising children.

Another way for me to explain what my parents were like would be by using two Bible stories that we hear in church. Luke 10:25-37 is the parable of the Good Samaritan. Jesus told His followers about how a good Samaritan had helped a man he found on the road after that man had been left for dead. In the story Jesus tells of how a priest, and a Levite had already passed by the man. My father would be like the Good Samaritan by helping another in that situation. While he would never have put his family in danger by stopping late at night if we were with him; he would find a way to help another person that is in need of assistance. The story that follows in Luke 10:38-42 can be used to explain what my mother was like. In this Bible story, while Jesus is visiting with two sisters Martha and Mary he was doing some teaching. Mary sat at the feet of Jesus to listen while Martha was preparing a meal for the guests. Martha mentioned the fact that she could use some help with the meal but Jesus told her that Mary had made the better choice. My Mother would be more like Martha preparing the meal but she would also listen to the Lord. In other words my mother would be both Martha and Mary. At times this passage is hard for me to wrap my mind around making a choice between necessary works or listening to the Lord. There has to be balance in life. I was always taught that true wealth is found within God, but someone does have to cook the meal and do the dishes.

After Mom was gone it became Dad's responsibility to get Christmas and birthday presents. Dad enjoys taking us out to eat for our birthday or he will make a meal at home. He has always been a good cook and he can even bake. For Christmas one year Dad got necklaces for his four daughters. He was telling me about them and I know he was pleased with what he had found. Yes, I did get to see them early; but it turns out all four of us got to see them ahead of time. Dad just had to share the gift early. The necklace was a heart with a small rose in the center. Inscribed on the back was:

"My little girl yesterday, my friend today, my daughter forever." He couldn't find anything quite as nice for the boys so they got money that year. All six of us were very pleased with our Christmas presents that year. Needless to say we are happy with every Christmas that Dad can celebrate with us.

A few more thoughts before I close this chapter: "Families are like fudge; Mostly sweet with a few nuts." My sister

Nancy and I both have a plate hanging on our wall with this saying. That is all I'll say about nuts in or out of my family.

In a church bulletin back in 2007 I found the following six statements about being thankful for the lives we have. My husband isn't impressed with all the numbers but the statements do give one an opportunity to consider how good their life is.

**If you wake up tomorrow with more health than illness, you are more blessed than the million who will not survive the week.

**If you have never experienced the danger of battle, the loneliness of imprisonment, the agony of torture or the pangs of starvation, you are ahead of 500 million people around the world.

**If you attend a church meeting without fear of harassment, arrest, torture or death, you are more blessed than almost three billion people in the world.

**If you have food in your refrigerator, clothes on your back, and a roof over your head and a place to sleep, you are richer than 75% of this world.

**If you have money in the bank, in your wallet, and spare change in a dish someplace, you are among the 8% of the world's wealthy.

**If you hold your head up with a smile on your face and are truly thankful, you are blessed because the majority can, but don't.

Another thing I found out when trying to put this book together; people have very different ways of remembering the SAME event. As my sisters and brothers were telling me "their take" on different events where I was involved, I realized they had a little different perspective than me. Let it be said: I am doing the writing and I am the oldest, their input has been requested and used, and here is our family story in black and white for posterity. Someone remembers what you will be reading the way it has been written in this book.

One last thought for chapter one:
Imagine if trees gave off WiFi signals, we would be planting so many trees we would probably save the planet. Too bad, they only produce the oxygen we breathe.

2/ More Time than Money

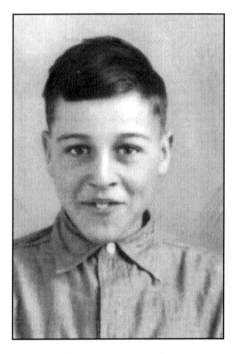

Dad was born in 1925 so we are thinking he is about 10 years old in this picture. He and Uncle Louie milked cows when they were 8 & 9 years old, that means this little guy had 2 years of experience at milking cows at the time this picture was taken.

After talking to Dad about his childhood I realize how much I have always taken for granted. My life is very comfortable because of what those that have gone before me did. We spend more money today on cell phones and TV hook-ups in a month than Dad's parents spent on their farm in a year. This last statement might be over exaggerated but I know people could spend less and still be happy back in the 1920's and 30's. Dad's family knew how to be happy with what they had which was very little. After working on this book about our family and the home Dad and Mom worked hard to establish for us, I realize how good our lives are now because of their efforts. My conclusion is that the happiest of people don't have the best of everything; they just make the most of everything they have.

Dad's mother, Margaret (Loerzel) Schmitt and his older sister, Loretta (Schmitt) Schramer did a lot of work to record the Schmitt family history. They would share what they wrote at the Schmitt family reunions, which were held on the Sunday after Father's day for more than 40 years. In recent years the Elburn location was no longer available to us so we have made a change. The reunions have been held at Uncle John's farm and in 2013 we celebrated John's 80th birthday at the same time as the family reunion.

The following paragraph was taken directly from Dad's document: Memories of Ralph (Pat) Schmitt Sr.

"It is really amazing the lives that are connected together by marriages from different parts of the country or I really should say all over the world. We should begin with my grandparents on my father's side who are the only ones I knew. Louis Schmitt was born in Kleinhausen, Germany on September 18, 1863. He came to the United States at the age of 16 in 1879. He came to Wheaton, Illinois. He was naturalized in DuPage County on October 24, 1888. Louis married Katherine Mittman who lived in Wheaton. Katherine was born October 23, 1863. They had four children: Mary, born in 1889; John, (my father), born in 1891; Albert, born in 1892; and Louis Jr., born in 1894. Louis (my grandfather) was in a wheelchair in the last years of his life. I remember visiting my grandparents and I would push him around and they would watch so I would not go too fast. My grandfather was about 70 years old when he passed on which was considered elderly for the early 1900's."

Dad's mother's parents lived in Perham, Minnesota. Grandma's father, Gustav Loerzel was born in Batavia on November 22, 1858 but moved to Minnesota when he was a teenager. He married Katherine Weirhus who was born on September 22, 1863. These are the grandparents that Dad never met because he never traveled to Minnesota nor did they travel to Illinois for a visit. Their daughter, Margaret, who was Dad's mother; moved to Aurora when she was 13 years old. She came to work for a family as a cook. She met John Schmitt and they married on October 7, 1913. While reading Dad's story and talking to him it made me realize how fortunate I was to know all four of my grandparents. When he said he only knew his paternal grandparents I thought his mother's parents had died. But it was a matter of traveling that made it difficult in those days to visit relatives that lived hundreds of miles away. Dad believes that when his mother left Minnesota to work in Illinois as a young teenager she seldom saw her parents again. He knows they wrote letters back and forth but visiting was made difficult because of the cost and distance. Letters were important in those early days and now in the 21st century that is becoming a lost form of communication.

Dad's parents, John and Margaret were the Grandparents that I lived with for a semester while I was in college. I used their address as my home address when my parents moved to Wisconsin. I did not move with them because I would have lost my Illinois teaching scholarship and would have had to pay out-of-state tuition. Grandpa and Grandma were living in DeKalb at that time.

My Mother didn't know any of her grandparents because her parents, Anton and Helen Eder were both born in Germany and came to the United States in their late teen years. Mom's maternal grandparents were Joseph and Katherine (Kreipl) Bircheneder. Her maternal great-grandparents were Joseph and Elizabeth (Walchshofer) Bircheneder. Her maternal great-great grandparents were Philip and Elizabeth Walchshofer. Mom's paternal grandparents were Herr(Mr.) Josef and Frau(Mrs.) Maria Eder. Her mother, Helen Eder had recorded these names for me when she and I were talking about her life in Germany and I did some research to verify the names using information from relatives that still live in Germany.

Grandma Eder told me she taught herself to speak English. When I studied German for a year I realized why she didn't write as well as she spoke when using the English language. In the German language, if one is talking about a red wagon it is translated as "wagon red"; the adjective is placed behind the noun. Grandma would talk about a red wagon but if she was writing about it, it was referred to as a wagon red. Now

I understand why she seemed to speak English better than when she was writing.

Mom's parents lived on a farm in Maple Park, Illinois, where our family lived for many years before we moved to Wisconsin. They also owned two bars; first one was in Compton and the second was in the Earlville. I can remember the second one better because we were older. When my youngest brother tells his cashew story the second bar in Earlville is where his story takes place. At one point Grandpa added an extra room onto that bar just for our family to visit. Now, years later I realize that it was a banquet room and it was also added to improve his business. They never owned more than one bar at a time. Grandma was a perfect bar owner because she truly enjoyed visiting with people. Grandpa Eder; on the other hand, was an introvert and was pleased just to listen to others interact.

Dad's grandparents, Louis and Katherine farmed near Aurora, Illinois in the early 1900's. They did everything by hand without the modern machinery that is used today. Aurora was a growing town because of the Fox River that ran through it and the surrounding towns. Dad explained that there was a dam built north of Aurora by Elgin, which made Aurora and the surrounding towns grow even faster. Today if you search for information about that dam and others that were built years ago you'll find information about using them for recreation. They were built to generate power for electricity, which some still do but the rivers are now used for exercise. Dad's grandparents worked on the farm without the use of modern machinery and had no need for exercise. Today we all have to put time aside in our day to exercise because of the modern conveniences we have, what a difference 100 years or more makes.

On February 7, 1933 Louis Schmitt past away so Katherine moved to Virgil to live with her daughter Mary and her husband William Reuland. They lived on a farm south west of Virgil, which had formerly been owned by William's brother Jake Reuland. I remember getting a note from Great-Grandma Katherine thanking me for a valentine I had made for her when I was in second grade. She wrote that my parents must be very proud of me. Guess it must have been a nice valentine. Dad described his Grandma Katherine as a strong willed woman. She had cataract surgery on one eye, which put an end to her crocheting and needlework. After that surgery she was not to move her head for 24 hours so sandbags were placed on either side of her head to prevent movement. Dad remembers when he stayed over night at her home that she put a tablespoon of vinegar in a glass of milk before going to bed, this would sour the milk and in the morning she would drink it. Dad thinks he was about 8 years old when he witnessed this event. Not that I would ever try this but Great-Grandma was 95 years old when she died on December 20, 1958. Just recently I saw an advertisement that claimed vinegar is better than many prescription drugs. There was a book to order for $25.00, which offers 1000 remedies for all kinds of human issues. I didn't place an order but when I get closer to 95 I'll consider it. I would have been 10 years old when Great-Grandma died. Both she and her husband, Louis are buried at Mount Olivet Cemetery in Aurora, Illinois.

Dad was born on Tuesday, November 24, 1925; just four days later on Saturday night, November 28th, The WSM

Barn Dance made its radio debut. This was later known as the Grand Ole Opry. (Just a little trivia for any of those trivia buffs.) As a child Dad remembers living on three different farms with his parents. They didn't own any of the farms so when they moved; it was usually done in late winter or early spring so they could be settled for spring planting. Also there would be less feed to move at that time of the year. When Dad was born they lived south of Virgil on the Michael Then farm, which was about 50 acres. The income on the farm came from milk, cream, eggs and poultry. They could sell these products or trade them for items at the grocery store. Dad's family planted a large vegetable garden where they grew radishes, lettuce, cabbage, beats, peas, green beans, cucumbers, and squash.

The stove used to make the meals was a wood stove. It had four lids on the top where pans could be placed to do the cooking. There was a reservoir in the back where water was warmed while the cooking was being done. This would be the water for washing dishes after the meal was completed. Dad mentions more than once about how good of a cook his mother was; she could make some delicious food using that wood stove without a control panel for the heat. Dad liked the end or crust of a freshly baked loaf of bread, which is also my favorite. He explained that they buttered this bread with butter that was churned from sweet cream. With 12 brothers and sisters he couldn't have always gotten the crust but he was in the middle of the family so for the years he was the baby in the family he might have gotten most of them. You know, somebody has to eat the rest of the loaf. The apple pies his mother made were also a favorite of his which were the best when eaten warm just out of the oven.

By March 1st of 1928 all the moving was completed and the family was now north of Virgil on the Jake Reuland farm. This was the second farm, which was behind the little general store. It was a larger farm with about 80 acres. Dad's sister Esther was born on the 16th of that month just two weeks after that move. This is one of the places my parents lived with me when I was a baby but I only remember being told about the place, I do not remember living in that location. We found a picture of Dad soaking his feet in a small tub of warm water in a kitchen. When I asked him about that picture he explained it was at this farm when we lived there about 1948 or 1949; that might be the only picture that we have of the farm behind the store.

Dad recalls that the summers of 1932 and 1933 were difficult years on the farm because of the extreme heat and lack of rain. This was when the Dust bowl devastated the Great Plains region of the United States. The great Depression (1929-1939) was also a part of our national history during those years. Dad's family did not have to abandon their farms like some families. Dad explained they were able to cut brush from the ditches to keep their animals feed.

When Dad wrote about the small town of Virgil where he grew up, I could picture some of the places he was describing, but I don't remember it the way he does. That is the difference of 20-plus years. When he was a boy there was a factory where farmers took their cans of milk to be shipped to Chicago. Grandpa John hauled three to six cans every day to the factory. Milking the cows in the 1930's was done by hand. That milk was put through a strainer and into the cans to be cooled and a windmill would pump the water to be used to cool the milk, if there was no wind then the water was pumped by hand; labor-intensive work. That factory; where Grandpa sold his milk, was closed when I was around Virgil but it was fun to use the hill where the factory was to slide down in the winter.

The small town of Virgil had a grocery store and post office in the same building. There was a bank located next door but closed after it was robbed around the 1920's. This was before there was such a thing as FDIC, which was established on January 1st, 1934. There was an implement dealer in early years that did eventually sell tractors. Those tractors and other supplies would come by railroad from Chicago.

For 30 years in the late 1800's the Virgil parish was a mission of St Mary's in Maple Park. The first church and school were built south of town located by the cemetery. When I was telling Dad and his brothers about this location, which is about two miles from the current church; they don't remember that location; they only remember the current one. There is a good reason because the current church was built in 1909 with the corner stone being placed by Bishop Muldoon that June; this was years before Dad's family moved to the area. As a child Dad was a member of St Peter & Paul Parish while Mom's family were members of St Mary's in Maple Park.

All eight grades were educated at St Peter & Paul parish school. Dad remembers walking to school but he didn't say it was uphill both ways, or that the snow was up to his knees. When we attended that school Mom drove us because we lived six miles from Virgil. The nuns from St Francis of Assisi order taught at the school. When the weather was cold or rainy the school had a large hall for the children to use for recess. We all attended this school; except Albert who had just finished kindergarten when we left for Wisconsin. Dad graduated from the school in 1940, I graduated in 1962, Pat in 1964, and Pam in 1967. But Dad went to the older school while his children; years later, attended the third school, which was newly built in 1953. There was also a public school in Virgil, which Dad showed me a few years ago. I knew it as the home of a classmate of mine, Cheryl Hardt. Dad does remember one day when they were already at school when one of the nuns asked all the children to pray for Sterling Bates, a classmate of theirs. A train had hit him that morning on his way to school. Later it was learned that the little guy had been trying to free his bike because a tire had gotten wedged in the tracks. Dad said the family didn't have much and he must have been desperate to save his bike. It just didn't work out for the boy and he was killed. How did that affect his family or even the conductor of the train? Their lives were forever changed and it was a difficult lesson about life.

When I was in grade school the nuns told us we had to be baptized to go to heaven and we HAD to be baptized in the Catholic Church. Some of my classmates took the information very seriously when they explained the concept to a non-classmate that was of another faith. That child was in tears by the time my classmates were finished explaining the after life to her. Catholics can be like that from time to time; some believe only Catholics can be saved. We also asked if animals could go to heaven but were told you need a soul and only humans have a soul. I'm no animal lover but this was another bit of information that some of my classmates found upsetting. Really? No animals or flowers in heaven?

In March of 1941 Dad and his family moved to the third farm where he lived with his parents. Grandma had all 12 of her children at the time of this move but a family tragedy loomed. This is the only farm I remember because they were living there while I was in grade school. It was south of Virgil and owned by William Schramer. This place was twice as large with 160 acres of tillable land and allowed the family to have 45 cows. Dad told me he and his older brother Louie milked the cows when they were 8 & 9 years old respectively. Dad explained that it was on this farm that they started milking with machines instead of by hand. They used surge buckets that would hang from a strap that was placed over the cow's back. With four units or buckets they were able to complete the milking in one and a half hours. Because they were using buckets the milk still had to be strained and carried to the milk house where it was cooled. There was no TV but then there would not have been time to watch TV.

Dad was the sixth child in his family; there were four girls and one boy before him. His oldest sister Katherine was 10 years older than him. She went to grade school in Virgil and then continued her education at a hospital in Aurora. He thinks she started working as an assistant nurse right after grade school and didn't think she went to high school. Kay married Raymond McDonald and they lived in Indianapolis, Indiana. Raymond did different odd jobs in the area, one of which was buying cars that were wrecked and in need of repair. After he would fix them up they would be ready to sell. Raymond and Katherine had five children. These were cousins that we knew because of the family reunions in the summer. One of their children, Jerold became a Capuchin priest. Just before I headed off to college, we went to visit him in the seminary. Another priest inquired about what I was planning to study. I explained that Physical Education was the field I planned to follow. He asked if I didn't think I should major in something more intellectual. Apparently he didn't know about all the science I would need to take for that degree. Father Jerry explained to him that "she is a farm girl; she'll be fine with Physical Education." Jerry made a very good priest because of his non-judgmental ways and his acceptance of people at their level. He was the priest that married my husband and me. At every family reunion he would always inquire if we were still married. The answer was and still is "yes." My parents did visit Kay's family but I don't think our entire family would make the trip. I only traveled to see them once by plane when Dad got his private pilot's license. The reason we flew to visit them was because Sylvia was making her First Communion. I don't remember the name of the church but it was huge. Now that I look back it was because I was usually going to the small church in Virgil.

Elizabeth was the second sister in the family. We called her Aunt Betty. Dad can remember that her husband, John was an excellent hunter. Dad explained that John always came back with something when he went hunting. If Dad went hunting with John, he was told to stay close and in front of John. That was the way John kept track of his little sidekick. This was when Dad was only about 6 years of age. Aunt Betty and John had four children. John was a farmer in Virgil for a few years but moved to other locations in Illinois.

Once when someone said something about Frances I didn't know whom he or she was talking about because the third child in Dad's family was called Fran. Dad said when Fran married George Altepeter it was a surprise to the family because he was much older than her. They had six children and lived in Virgil. I remember Fran always being in the nicest mood with the most pleasant smile and had a positive outlook on life even into her later years. She was active well into her 80's and enjoyed life. Her first child, Loretta lived only a few months. Her other five adult children wrote a book in 2012. The title is <u>Fluffy, Funny, and Fabulous, a tale of five sisters.</u> For the Christmas of 2012, Dad purchased 7 copies; one for himself and all six of his offspring. One of the reviews I read explained you would want to be part of their family after reading the book. That review is correct. The book gave wonderful insights into a happy family's home life.

Aunt Loretta and her husband Matthew lived on a farm near Virgil. I remember visiting them on that farm and having lots of enjoyable times wandering in the buildings and on the land. The house was huge because there were three stories. I don't remember the arrangement of the rooms, because we didn't spend much time inside, we played outside. There were seven children in the family. At one point Uncle Mat decided to move to Virgil where they built a new home. It was only a few blocks from our school. Actually it was between that third farm of my Grandparents and the school. Grandpa's farm was just out of the town limits. We must have walked home with my cousins a few times because we did walk to Grandma's if Mom was going to be late to pick us up. This is the family that organized a school reunion of all the classes from St Peter & Paul school which closed in 1971. Their daughter, Sue arranged to have each class picture taken, which made a nice keepsake for all that attended.

Next in the order of birth was Uncle Louie, who arrived in 1924 a year before Dad. He and Dad worked together hauling insulation to factories and contractors. This was a business started by Uncle Louie after he had worked for some farmers at the beginning of his working career. Dad and Louie; sometimes called Chuck looked alike. This doesn't seem unreasonable because they were brothers, but it was uncanny how much they resembled each other. Once when they arrived together at a place where they were working as truck drivers a man looked so surprised and made the comment, "that is why you can haul out and back so fast, there are two of you." That man would see Louie come in with a load and after unloading leave only to return in a few hours with another load. He just didn't realize the second guy was my Dad until he saw the two brothers together. Another time Christy, a granddaughter of Dad's went to Uncle Louie and wanted to be picked up. She was about 2 years old at the time. She was pleased to be up high to see what was going on around the room. At one point she spotted Dad, her Grandpa. She took one look at Uncle Louie and realized she didn't want to be with him, got down, and headed across the room for her Grandfather. According to family folklore this happened to more than just Christy. One of Uncle Louie's grandchildren went to Dad thinking he was her Grandfather. In 1955 Uncle Louie was involved in a very serious trucking accident. He would not have lived except for the miracle that took place that night. His truck broke down on a busy four-lane highway and a tow truck was called. Louie was between the two trucks when a third semi slammed into the rear truck. Uncle Louie's guardian angel had an ambulance stop even before he was found under the rear wheels. He would have bleed to death in a matter of minutes if they had had to call an ambulance and wait for its

25

arrival. Louie had a rough few months in recovery but when he went back to work he was a dispatcher for the company. Louie and his family moved to Loyal, Wisconsin in 1959 to do some farming. They were there during the years Dad had his own plane and Uncle Louie's farm was another place we flew for a visit. We landed in a field instead of going to an airport. Years later when our family moved to Wisconsin Louie's family had returned to Virgil, Illinois. Uncle Louie had a son, Larry that was one of the triplets, which is a story to follow when I write about Uncle John.

Ralph Frank Schmitt arrived on November 24, 1925. I find it interesting that when you look at Dad's baptismal certificate his middle name is listed as Francis but he insists his middle name is Frank. When Dad was young, his father had a hired man named Mike. His last name has been forgotten over the years. Dad was about 4 years old and he would follow this hired man around as Mike was doing his chores. Mike gave little Ralph the nickname of Pat; so they were Mike and Pat. That nickname has stayed with Dad to this day. Once someone asked Dad if Ralph Schmitt was related to Pat Schmitt. Yes they are, thanks to Mike.

Dad's sister Esther lived in Sycamore and was a wonderful seamstress. She would make lots of her clothes as well as her children's. She would also sew and mend for other people. Word of mouth was her only means of advertising and there was plenty of sewing to keep her busy. Aunt Esther was a classmate of my mother's in high school. Esther was the first one in her immediate family to graduate from high school. She and Vern Warber had four children after they married in 1947. Vern worked for the post office and had a route to walk everyday that allowed him to stop at home for a coffee break.

I remember how cold he looked one winter day when we were visiting. Snow, wind, rain: nothing stopped him from delivering the mail. Their daughter, Donna was another one of the triplets.

Next Grandpa and Grandma had a set of twins. Nicholas and Margaret were Christmas babies in 1929. Nicholas was born with asthma, which was not as treatable in 1929 as it is now. I remember Aunt Esther saying that his feather pillow would have been part of the problem but no one knew that when he was growing up. Dad said Nicky missed a lot of school in the fall because his breathing was most difficult during the summer and fall. The first tragedy that the family had to endure was the loss of their brother Nicky. He passed away on June 15, 1941 just after his 12th birthday. Dad explained that Nicky's classmates came to their home to pay their last respects because that is where the wake was held. What a sad time for the entire family but Margaret must have been devastated after losing her twin brother. I only knew Margaret as Sis; it wasn't until I was in college that I realized her name was Margaret and she was her mother's namesake. She was married to Bernard Bewsey and they had seven children.

Jean was the tenth child to be born. She and George Ramer married in 1951 and had three children. I remember Jean was always helping Grandpa and Grandma in their later years. When they moved off the farm and lived in the DeKalb area they were close to Jean and her family. Jean would take Grandma shopping or to get her hair done. Grandma never learned to drive and Grandpa didn't drive in DeKalb once the town grew and the streets were so busy with the newer, faster cars. While talking to Aunt Jean I learned that she, Sis and Esther were the only ones in the family to graduate from high school. The high school was in Maple Park, which was about five miles away. Dad thought everyone after him had gone on to high school. Uncle John and Uncle Bob started but they both assured me they were not interested in four years of higher education.

John was next; he was the only son that Grandpa and Grandma had that was in the service. He went into the Marines after dropping out of high school. He said they didn't have enough women and they didn't pay as much as they do today. He was in the service during the Korean conflict, which he said was not called a war from 1950 to 1953 when it was being fought. I did some research and found that today it is referred to as the "The Forgotten War" because of the lack of attention it received in the 1950's. Harry S Truman, who was the President at the time called it a "police action" because it was directed under the United Nations. John told us about some moonshine that they made while stationed in the Mediterranean Sea. Sounds like that TV show; MASH was based on his life. He explained that they made apple jack in a container made of lead. When their moonshine went through the fermenting process lead was drawn into the alcohol from that container. When the troops started drinking the moonshine they ended up very sick but nobody went to sickbay. They most likely had lead poisoning and could have died. He made it through the service and the moonshine to come home and marry Diane. They raised four children together. He was the Godfather to the triplets. I have to explain we were not really triplets. We were all born within 3 weeks of each other and at family reunions I was told they had to take pictures of the triplets. The triplets were Donna, Esther's daughter; Larry, Louie's son, and me.

I do have the picture of the three of us when we turned 50. Larry's sense of humor was something else. When we saw each other at the reunion in 1998, he asked, "How does it feel to finally be old?" I always liked my cousin Larry until he started calling me old.

The baby in Dad's family was Robert who was born in 1935, once the baby it seems like it is impossible to shake that label but Uncle Bob never seemed to be that young to be considered a baby to me. He and his wife, Janice raised four children. Bob worked on the farm at home but later became a construction worker. He built several of the homes where his family lived. Bob told me that in 1949 it became the law that you could not quit school until you were 16 years of age. John and Bob must have been caught by the law and needed to at least start high school. Back in those days it was still possible to get a good job and support your family without a high school diploma, which everyone in Dad's family were able to accomplish.

Now back to Grandpa and Grandma's farm that remains in my memory. They remained on this farm for more than 20 years, only to move when Grandpa retired from farming. The front door that I went in as a child was on an enclosed porch, which lead into the large kitchen. Off to the right was the living room and beyond that was the sitting room that had double doors which were usually closed. The only time I remember going into the sitting room was at Christmas time when we were told to sit in front of the Christmas tree and Grandpa would bring in our Christmas present. It was always a huge basket of fruit, which now I realize was a bushel basket. When the clear plastic paper was pulled off we could eat our fill of the fruit. On the top were the best grapes, which was all I selected to eat. There were nuts sprinkled around the rest of the fruit. Bananas, pears, and plums were on top and the bottom two thirds were red and green apples. For at least two weeks after Christmas we could still get an apple when we went to Grandma's home. She always gave the best hugs to go with those apples.

When I was telling Dad about my memory of those Christmas baskets he explained that was where his brother Nicky was laid to rest after he died at the age of 12. Someone from the family remained with him through the night to keep vigil. Grandpa and Grandma had lost one of their precious children to asthma. If Nicky were living today medication would help him deal with this condition.

There are many wonderful memories of that third farm; one of which is the tall mulberry tree in the front yard. During the summer or early fall when the berries were ripe it was fun to eat your fill until you had purple fingers; try as hard as I could, never would I come away from that tree with clean fingers if the berries were ripe. The berries were low enough for us to pick them from the ground but I still enjoyed getting up on the lower branches to see how much more I could reach. Another thing I remember was eating hard-boiled eggs with my cousin Donnie Sauber, Aunt Betty's son. He was 20 years older than me and stayed with our grandparents during the summer to help with the haying and other farm chores. Every once in a while he would get a hard-boiled egg out of the refrigerator, pick up a salt shaker and tell me to follow. Out we would go to sit under that mulberry tree and share the egg. He liked the whites and I ate the yokes. If I ever develop high cholesterol it will be because of Donnie.

When I was young and visiting my Grandparents I remember Grandma Schmitt fixing breakfast in the morning and then after the dishes were washed and put away she would go in the living room to kneel by a chair and say the rosary. I remember thinking that I planned to be as holy as she was when I got to be her age. If I were 10 at the time she would have been about 64 years old. The jury is still out as to if I am there or not. I'll keep striving to be more like my Grandma Schmitt because I am in that age group now.

My Mom's family never collected the data like Dad's family did, so I don't have the dates of individual's births, marriages, or deaths. I plan to do some research and put a document together but I do need to retire and start writing and researching as a career. We all have the same 24 hours in a day but why does it seem that others can get so much more completed in a day and I seem to be spinning my wheels. In 2011 I spent about 2 hours in the library working with an ancestry program that you have to use when you are in the library. It gave me an opportunity to research public records for my four Grandparents. This program, ancestry. com gave me access to the 1930 census. I found my father listed as a four-year old. Using it in the library means I don't have to purchase the program. I could see myself buying the program and never using it enough to justify the purchase price; thus the reason I'll work in the library. Now I'll move on to Mom's sisters and brother along with some of my memories of them.

Mom's family starts with Helen who was the oldest in the family. She was born in Germany and didn't come to this country until she was five years old. She and her husband, Bud Studebaker raised five children during their marriage.

31

He was injured in the war when he was in the service, which later caused cancer. He was a hard worker all his life and had many different jobs to support his family. Helen went into nursing and went back to that career once her children were in school. I remember one beautiful spring day when I was about 10 years old. We were playing softball in their backyard. It is where my cousins always played ball but when I connected with a pitch I broke a window. Helen came out to see what was happening and since no one was hurt just told us to move away from the house. I was never told to pay for the window but then my only job at the time was going to school. Dad must have covered it because Dads do that kind of thing. Guess I was really a "hitter" when I was young.

My Mom, Mary Margaret was the second born in the family. It is my understanding that, when she was young, her relatives called her Mary Margaret. I didn't find this out until after Mom had died but I believe her sisters called her Mary, while her aunts and uncles referred to her as Mary Margaret. We found letters that were written to Mom where she was addressed as "Mary Margaret." Each of the six children that Mom raised has a chapter to follow this one.

Next was Eleanor who married Chuck Stowe and raised three boys. He worked for the post office for many years. Once when visiting their family, she showed me her music box collection. She had started the collection as the boys were growing up because it was something they could get for her as a gift for occasions like birthdays, Mother's day or Christmas. She had many interesting boxes and a story to go with most of them. Eleanor and her husband purchased her parents' tavern when Grandpa and Grandma were ready to retire. While they owned it, Grandpa and Grandma had never been robbed but Eleanor and Chuck were robbed at gunpoint shortly after they purchased the tavern. It was a frightening experience and the bar was then sold within months.

Uncle Bud was the baby in the family. His real name was Anton Jr. He worked with Grandpa and Grandma when they had the bar. He also worked part time for the post office until later when he was employed full time as a postal worker. He and Barb raised two children; Greg and Karen. They had another baby between Greg and Karen that was called back to heaven after less than two years on this earth. It was a car accident that took Gwen from us. I remember my little sister Pam, who was only 8 years old at the time we lost Gwen. Pam just burst into tears when we got in the car to go to the cemetery after the funeral. It was a baby crying for the loss of another baby. Karen was such a beautiful surprise after that tragedy.

I remember asking Dad how I was to going to repay him and Mom for all they had done for me over the years. He explained that I couldn't; but when I have children of my own, I just do for them what was done for me. His parents, as well as Mom's must have been great role models because Mom and Dad were kind, loving parents. They created a family home for us that made us feel like we were the center of the universe. Years later my son asked me the same question when he was in college. I told him what his Grandpa told me just pay it forward by making a good home for your own kids. At their wedding dinner he mentioned in his speech that he was not sure he could carry on the tradition. He and his wife Sarah have raised the bar yet again, and they are wonderful parents.

When I was talking to Dad about what he is doing now I asked about his duties in city government in Loyal. He said he has been weed commissioner for six years and plans to continue another two years. I asked if those two years depend on if he wins the next election. "I already won," was his reply. It is hard to keep up with him and I don't get to vote in Loyal. The last time we saw Uncle Bob he asked if Dad was still the mayor of Loyal. Dad was asked to run as mayor but he feels he is doing just fine as an alderman and dealing with weed control in town. Later in Ralph JR's chapter you can read "the rest of the story" about my Dad as a lady's man, which will be chapter six.

3/If you obey all the rules; you'll miss all the fun

This is the Christmas picture for 2013. It was taken at Sarah's parents' cottage while Kevin's family was visiting Wisconsin. Left to right: Valerie, Kevin, Andrew, Connie, Sarah, holding Parker, and Raymond.

It was important to our parents that we be raised as Catholics. I remember being outside at my Grandparents' farm in Virgil when Mom told me that the priest approved her request to have me attend St. Peter & Paul. We were living in Maple Park and should have been going to the church in that community but we had joined the one in Virgil because of the Catholic grade school. Religion and grammar were the most important areas taught by the nuns. Religion makes sense and grammar was used in all other subject areas. We were expected to use full sentences even when writing for a history paper. When I was in grade school I was a very good little Catholic girl.

If Mom called me "Constance Mary" I knew I was in trouble. Hard to believe; isn't it, if you refer to what I wrote in the last paragraph? Because I am the first-born I had my parents all to myself for a year and a half before Patricia came along. I don't remember any of this quality time but I am sure I was treated just like the others were in later years. We lacked nothing because we all knew our parents loved us and would do anything for us.

My birth date was always celebrated on June 7th until I requested a copy of my birth certificate when I got married. To my surprise it said I was born on June 6th. My mother explained she went to church on Sunday, June 6th, 1948. Much later in the day she went to the hospital and I was born after midnight. Check a calendar from 1948; if you didn't save one "google it," as my Dad would say. The birth certificate has the time right but the date is wrong. Now everybody is confused but me; my passport has to say June 6th and I have been forced to celebrate both days. Life is tough but it is a cross I must bear.

My first memory was when I was in kindergarten. I went to the public school that first year because we lived in Elburn. I remember never getting anything marked wrong on my papers that first year. School was really easy for me. There were three of us at the time because Pam was born while I was in kindergarten. We were going to be moving to Maple Park but I was enrolled in the parish school in Virgil. There was no bus to take me to school so Mom drove me to and from school each day. I am sure that really broke up her day. School had been so easy the year before and I remember being crushed when I got my first mistake on a paper in first grade. Guess I wasn't as smart as I thought I was because it was a wake up call; pay attention.

That home in Elburn is actually the first one I remember. It was the third place that my parents lived according to Dad. I don't remember the first two, which were both in Virgil. My Mom's parents owned the home where we moved to in Maple Park. We lived there until we moved to Wisconsin. Grandpa and Grandma Eder had been living in that home but they moved when they had purchased a bar. In Maple Park we had a barn where Dad raised a few beef cattle every year. There was a woods that gave us an opportunity to explore. There was a huge old tree that had a trunk that split into two large branches about 4 feet up, which created a great place to sit. I know we needed help to get up there but I don't remember what we used. I do remember sitting up there to read a book or just watch what was happening in the world. My Uncle Bud; Mom's youngest brother, told me that tree had been used as a point of reference on an Indian trail. I don't know how he found this out but it sounds like a great rural legend to me and that tree did have a very distinctive look.

I really always enjoyed going to school. When we were taught by the nuns at St Peter & Paul it was a common theme with all or at least most of the girls that we were going to become nuns. I remember Mom telling me that Dad thought I would make a good nun. We know that didn't happen but not because I wasn't qualified according to my father. St Peter & Paul Elementary was where I went to school from 1954 to 1962; first through eighth grades. The nuns were from the St Francis of Assisi order and they taught us during the earliest years but a teacher from the secular world started at our school around 1959 or 1960. Every morning before classes we attended Mass. Think of how many Masses that was. I would be a very holy person if I had paid close attention at each of those Masses. My mind would wonder and I did some of my best daydreaming during those Masses.

We always sat in the front of church with the youngest students being directly in front and the older students behind them. Makes sense; the little guys would not be able to see over the older taller students. A few times each month we would have a High Mass which meant there was Benediction. The additional service was at the end of the Mass in which we asked for God's blessing. At issue for me was that incense was used during this service. The smell bothered me so much; that I was sure I would pass out or throw up. This was especially bad when I was young because there I was right in front. I would leave Mass early and just hang out in back until the end of the service to join my classmates as they left to go to school.

One of the nuns talked to me about why I left early and I explained the situation. The next time it happened I was told that I was to ask my mother to come inside and talk to the nun about my behavior. When I went to the car that night after school, there was my Father. He never picked us up from school because he was always working. I have no idea why he was there that time but I told him he had to go in to talk to the nun. She explained to my Father that I was always leaving church early during Benediction. "Maybe she is allergic to church like I am," was his reply. I could have kissed him but I tried hard to show no reaction. I don't remember what those two adults decided but I continued to leave when incense was used for a few more times. As I got older and didn't sit so close and I was able to endure the fragrant odor. I never did pass out or lose my cookies during Benediction but I still don't care for the smell of incense.

For high school I went to Kaneland, which was considered a new school. That school was created when high schools in the small surrounding rural towns were consolidated to offer more opportunities to students. Some of these small towns were Elburn, Kaneville, Maple Park, Sugar Grove, and Virgil. When in high school I followed the "college" path which means when my Mom said I needed to take typing because she "wasn't going to type my papers in college" I needed her signature to take that as an extra class. It wasn't a requirement to get into college according to the school but Mom had the right idea. It is good that she was looking over my course work.

Being the oldest meant that I had to break the way for the others kids. Being a girl was not an advantage because boys get more freedom. I can remember the early curfew and my first high school dance where my date had to meet me at the dance. He could not pick me up at my home; my father drove me to the dance and picked me up after the dance. No discussion, that was the only way I was going to be able to attend the homecoming dance my freshman year. When I was a parent with children of my own; I wish I could have taken them back to a time like that, but then I didn't like it when I was living it.

I don't remember a lot about my first high school prom except the shopping I did with my Mom for the dress. We spent an entire morning going from store to store to find the perfect dress. I don't think I was that concerned about the dress; Mom was concerned about the cost. After lunch we found a very nice floor-length pink dress with white lace over the top. The bottom of the bodice and hem had scalloped edges, which really made the dress stand out. It was on sale for $9.00. My favorite color is red but pink is a very close second. The only problem was it was too long. Mom said if I took that dress she would shorten it, so we were done shopping but now the real work was to begin. Mom was very good at sewing and had passed that skill on to three of her four daughters. Pat, Pam, & I learned to sew from Mom as well as 4-H. Because of my sewing ability I would have just turned the hem up losing the scalloped edge at the bottom of the dress. Not my Mother; she took the dress apart in the middle meaning even the 18-inch zipper needed to be removed from the back of the dress. She took the extra inches out at the waist. Her efforts maintained the integrity of that beautiful dress.

My first job was babysitting. I do remember babysitting for Carol Nelson who was our 4-H leader. When I was in 4-H I didn't appreciate all the work that those leaders do; it became apparent to me once my kids were in 4-H and I found myself as a leader. Whenever I babysat I would make sure the house was locked and the shades were pulled down on all the windows. My worst fear was to look out a window and have someone looking back at me. Once I was babysitting for two sisters in Maple Park and I couldn't lock the back door; there was no lock. Just accept it, ignore it, and get the kids to bed was my decision. All went well until around 1AM when I was awakened by a noise. I had fallen to sleep while doing my homework. Not making any noise myself, I figured out the noise was coming from the kitchen. It sounded like someone going through the grocery bags that were left out on the floor. I said a silent prayer to the Lord and asked Him to protect me. I had actually made up my mind that I was ready to die. Imagine my relief when the family cat came walking into the living room. I had been positive that there was a person in the kitchen. I called my parents, in tears, to say I was OK. I just had to wake them up and let them know I wasn't dying today. I was explaining how it didn't matter that there wasn't a lock on the back door. Mom talked to me and assured me that Dad was on the way and I was to call her back when he arrived. So at 5 AM when those sisters finally returned home; there sat my father with me waiting for them. Dad just smiled and explained I got bored and he came to keep me company. It was getting light out when headed home. I'm not sure how much sleep Dad lacked but I went to bed when we arrived home. I don't remember ever babysitting for them again.

After my high school graduation I went to Northern Illinois University to major in physical education. It seems to me that my parents were always available to me and this was before we ever had cell phones. NIU, in DeKalb was only 25 miles from home but I stayed on campus. I didn't go home on weekends because I was working to be able to pay for next semester and then there was the studying to be completed. But I did call home a lot to check in and make sure they weren't missing me. However, once when I called home, no one answered the phone. I was sure there was something wrong, Mom didn't work outside the home and I was calling when my sisters and brothers should have been home from school. I was very worried until I finally got to talk to someone. Maybe those calls were more because I was missing them than the other way around.

When I was a freshman in college I worn the same prom dress I wore when I was in high school; that was my Mom's $9 purchase. I had a few other dresses in high school but that pink one was my favorite. Our dorm had some formal dance so I went with a boy that I had gone to high school with but never dated while in high school. He wore a nice suit and commented on how much all of the girls must have spent on our dresses only to wear them once. I didn't have the heart to tell him I was wearing mine for a second time and he might have been at the prom where I wore it the first time.

During my junior year of college I met Raymond Milz from Loyal, WI; where my parents lived at that time, that would have been the fall of 1968. We had been writing each other because his mother sent him my address. I had always been close to meeting Ray but just never did. The Milz family lived by my Uncle Louie when Louie's family was in Wisconsin; but when I visited Uncle Louie I didn't meet the neighbors. When Ray graduated from high school he wanted to work on a farm so Uncle Louie sent him to my Dad who hooked Ray up with Ron Hartman. Ron was a patron of Dad's on his milk route. Ray worked for Ron for a few years before he was drafted into the Army. But it took his mother to decide he should meet me and we started writing just about the time he was getting out of the service. Thus as the story goes; I graduated from NIU in June of 1970 and married Raymond that July. Our wedding day is one of those events where two people or more are involved and you come up with different stories. I thought it was a beautiful day while Ray is sure it was the hottest day that summer. I was there; the day was quite comfortable according to my memory.

Because NIU was located 50 miles west of Chicago it was assumed that I might get a job in or near Chicago. Many Physical Education majors who were being hired at those schools were asked to teach Driver Education. My minor was going to be math but I changed to Driver Education just to help improve my chances of getting a job. As it turned out, before I completed my education I did sign a contract to teach Physical Education in Marshfield. The plan was to teach for three years to earn my lifetime certification and then raise kids. After the kids would be in school I would start teaching again. That plan didn't work. Before my three years were completed, Raymond was farming and we realized that we needed health insurance. I liked my job and I didn't want much to do with farming. It worked out OK; I taught for 33 years while Raymond milked cows for 41 years. I never milked a cow in those 41 years; yet another regret I bear.

Our first child, Valerie was such an easygoing kid. When Val was about 5 or 6 years old Mom took her shopping and wanted to buy Val something. Mom loved to shop and Valerie was great company. Mom told her to pick something up for herself and Mom would pay for it. Mom explained it to me later that Val didn't want or need anything. That is my Valerie; she enjoys life and is happy with what she has.

Our next offspring, Kevin was a strong-willed individual. When he was about 3 or 4 he was helping Ray unload hay. Never mind the heavy bales; he could be on top of the load and see all the action while pushing one down for his Dad to put on the elevator. We were living in Milladore at the time. Millie and Rudy Younger lived on the farm across from us. They had always insisted the kids call them Grandpa and Grandma. When my parents stopped by and saw Ray working Dad headed toward the wagon to supervise. Just about that time Rudy came from his place so Dad and Rudy were walking toward the wagon together. From the top of the wagon Kevin yelled, Hi Grandpa." Both of them said hi; but I later asked Dad if he knew who Kevin was addressing? Dad assured me he knew and was not offended. It was just that my kids saw Millie and Rudy more than my parents.

Every mother wants to do things with her children. When my two kids were smaller it was easy to find an activity that they both enjoyed. Swimming was a favorite past time when we were looking for physical exercise. With an indoor pool at the high school where I taught, and an outdoor pool in Marshfield we had opportunities to swim. Both kids learned to swim at an early age but as they grew older they developed different interests. Valerie enjoyed less active things. She didn't mind being a spectator for different sports. Kevin, four years younger wanted to always be on the move. He had to be a player and didn't care to watch others play. As far as differences this was just the start. Going out for fast food; one wanted Hardees and the other McDonalds. "How about pie for dessert?" I would ask. One voted apple the other blueberry. Their father was no help. He was easy going and liked both apple and blueberry. So when they were fourteen and ten and I introduced them to skiing it was not a big surprise that one like downhill and the other cross-country. In Wisconsin these are a great winter sports.

Currently Valerie lives one mile from us and makes her home in Milladore. The house where she lives was built more than 100 years ago as a doctor's office. Later it was the home for the manager of the lumberyard, which was established in Milladore because of the location of the train tracks. She works at Kick-A-Poo cheese plant in Sherry; which means her morning commute to work is less than 5 miles. She usually goes with us on Friday nights to have a fish fry with Grandpa.

Kevin and his family live 900 miles from us in Kingsport, Tennessee and will soon re-locate in Chattanooga; this means they will be 30 miles closer to us. He and his wife, Sarah went to high school together and married after college. They have two boys; Andrew Matthew and Parker Thomas. Kevin works as a sales engineer for Hoffman-Hoffman in Johnson City, TN. Sarah is a registered nurse but at this time she is a stay-at-home Mom which means she "brings her work with her" during the summer to stay at her parents' home in Wisconsin for 6 weeks. That gives us a great opportunity to visit with the boys and they try to visit my Dad during those summer visits when Kevin and his family are in Wisconsin.

There was a little angel, Carson born to Kevin & Sarah, May 6th, 2005 but he was called back to heaven because Jesus needed another angel. Valerie was his Godmother. He was 2 ½ months old when he returned to heaven on July 20, 2005 to live with Jesus. It is hard for a parent to stand at the grave of their child, and it was hard to watch my son and his wife grieve for their first-born. We are thankful for the fact that

Jesus has overcome death, which means we will see our little Carson again someday.

Facebook gives me an opportunity to see pictures of my grandchildren and check on my two kids. Valerie posts recipes that are healthy while Kevin reflects on life. One of his recent posts was telling about two studies. He wrote, "A recent study found the average American walks 900 miles per year. Another study found that Americans drink, on average, 22 gallons of beer per year." His conclusion is that Americans, again considering averages; "get 41 miles to a gallon. Kind of makes you proud to be an American." Please don't think he came up with that stuff on his own. He just has the sense of humor like my father and wants to make others smile.

4/ Let Out The Clutch

Patricia's family: left to right: Stephanie holding son, Quentin: Josilyn, Braydon, Lisa; Kimberly with son Nathan in front; and Patricia.

Mom and Dad's second child, Patricia remembers baking with Mom who was a skilled cook. Patricia or Pat did a lot of baking for the fair in the summer time. We all belonged to the local 4-H club. Cooking and baking were projects that were favorites of Pat's when she participated in 4-H. While in high school, Pat didn't find the time to take Home

Economics because of requirements to get into college. Mom filled in where needed to make Pat a wonderful cook just like her mother. Now Pat has three children and four grandchildren who all enjoy her talent in the kitchen.

Patricia's favorite story about Dad was watching him on the slip-a-slide. Her exact words were; "you have to write about arms, butt, and legs flying." When we lived in Illinois on the farm in Maple Park Mom got us a slip-a-slide. It was a long narrow piece of plastic about 30 feet by 4 feet that we could hook a garden hose up to at one end. Water would run down the length of the slide to keep it slippery, with the plan being to get a running start and slide the length of the plastic. As I remember it that was not easy and the water was cold. Placement of the slide was important because a downhill slope in the lawn added to the ride. On hot summer days it was a lot of fun and we all tried our best to get the furthest. When Dad got home from work it didn't take much encouragement to get him to join the fun especially on a muggy day. When Dad would slide down his feet would be in the air while he was on his back. We loved watching him as he enjoyed the activity with us. Mom had the movie camera out and was recording all of the action for us. Later watching Dad on film was even funnier. Our parents were never worried about the lawn. We changed the placement of the slide every day because there always was a mud hole at the end of the slide after a few hours of fun. Dad assured us the lawn would grow back and it always did.

The next family folklore story is called "putting the pumpkin on the porch." I believe this story took place during the fall of 1964 or 1965. Just some background for this story; Mom had pet names for her youngest child, one of them being

"Pumpkin." It was going to be a cool evening and Mom wanted the Halloween pumpkin brought in and put on the front porch so it would not freeze. Maybe you as the reader are way ahead of me. Yes, when Mom said "put the pumpkin on the porch" Patricia picked up little Albert and put him on the porch. "Why is that kid crying?" Mom asked. I guess he didn't want to stay on the porch because even if he wasn't going to freeze there it was colder than the house. Patricia, seeing the error of her ways, let the kid go back to his toys and got the "other" pumpkin on the porch. We don't really know if Al was coming in from outside to be put on the porch or if he was inside the house already and was being sent to the porch. One thing we are sure of; you never picked on the little guy or Mom would not be a "happy camper." And we all know of the saying, "if mom isn't happy, there is no one happy."

My sister, Pat also wrote; "one thing I remember about Mom is she was always there for me in a pinch." She is correct; our parents were always there whenever any of the six of us needed help. Pat's memories continue:

"When we were in high school, we had to wear gym suits. When I would bring my gym suit down Sunday night after being crumpled in the corner and smelly all weekend, Mom would stay up to wash and iron it. I would come down Monday morning and there it would be all ready for me." Just to add a note; the reason Pat didn't give Mom her gym suit until Sunday night was because she didn't start her homework until Sunday night. If she would have started that homework on Saturday the gym suit could have been washed at that time. When Mom got one gym suit she asked for the others; but then no one started homework until the last minute. At least she had several to wash together and with six kids Mom could come up with a load of laundry at anytime day or night.

Pat wrote: "When I was in 4-H I signed up for sewing. I had to make an elastic waist skirt. I remember the material was this pretty pink and white small checks. On the last night before we had to turn it in, of course, procrastinator that I was, it was not completed. Next morning I get up and there it is all finished, looking beautiful. I am sure I received a blue ribbon. Of course then there was Dad. When Connie and I were in high school, Mom and Dad had a car for us to drive. For gas, all we had to do was back up to the gas pump on the farm and gas the car up. We didn't pay for the gas, insurance, or car. So one day after school, we called Dad to say, the car won't start. He asked, 'does it have gas?' We say, yes, it has gas. So dad comes over to our high school (with gas in gas can) and guess what. It was out of gas." Side bar here about this story. This happened in the winter and Dad had jumper cables just in case we did actually have gas and there was a dead battery. This was not the first time we couldn't start our car because it didn't have gas. We showed Dad the gas gauge that made it look like we had plenty of gas but we realized then it didn't work. After that incident we were told to use the odometer to put 200 miles on the car and then gas up. As Pat continues her story, she is correct with the assessment of our Father, he is a calm individual.

"I always remember Dad as being very calm. Must be where I get it. (Note: Pat? Calm? This is her being funny.) But we would be ready to go somewhere and we could not find something. He would very calmly say, where were you the last time you remember having it? I would think and could always find whatever I was looking for by just thinking instead of getting all excited and upset. Worked with shoes, clothes, keys etc. As an adult, I always tried using this with my kids too."

"I remember on the farm we had calves. They were always fun to feed with the little calf bucket. We also had ponies. I liked to ride the one that was really fat and old. (Forgot his name) I liked to ride him because he didn't go very fast on the way down to the woods. He did go slightly faster on the way home because he wanted to get home and rest." The woods Patricia is referring to, is where that great tree was that I liked to sit in and read. Now that she has reminded me of the pony, I know more than once I used the pony to help me get into the tree and maybe Pat headed home on the pony. To get down it was easy if you understand gravity; jump.

Dad remembers once when the electricity went off. We were all in the house for the evening and now what do you do? Get candles out and make sure you aren't going to start a fire, which will only make the situation go from bad to worse. Now that you can see by the candlelight, decide what you are going to do until bedtime. Your first two or three suggestions will most likely involve electricity. Dad thinks Pat was about 8 years old when she made the comment, "might as well be dead." She was a drama queen but after she grew out of that stage there was Nancy who took up that part.

Pat remembers when Dad started flying that our Mother was not a big fan. She would go with him if he was flying to Wisconsin or Indiana but short trips around Illinois were not for her. She didn't care to go up just to view the world below but her kids would fly with Dad anytime. Pat recalls that the smell of airplane fuel could be strong and the odor did bother her. Another odor that can get to her is the smell of cigar smoke, which could get to a person if they were riding with Dad in the truck. On one particular occasion she went with Dad for a plane ride and the odor of the fuel made her nauseous. Dad's patience was very evident to her that day when he just cleaned up the mess she made because she did get sick because of the fumes. After that event Dad found some burp bags for us and showed us where they were located before take-off. But Pat is right; Dad was always patient with his kids.

Before we go on to Patricia's next story I have to tell you about her career as a detasseler when she was in high school. To develop hybrid corn two types of corn are planted in one field. Using both specialized machines and human labor several rows of one variety or type are detaseled which means the tassel on the top of the corn is taken off and dropped on the ground. The field of corn was then pollinated by only one variety resulting in a hybrid. Pat would get up very early in the morning for this job, which lasted 3 to 4 weeks in the summer. She sat on a machine with 5 other people and pulled the tassels off the corn as a seventh person drove the machine through the corn. I am sure it is because she was always on time for the job and showed a high level of responsibility that she received a promotion the second year. She became the driver. This makes her next story so much more interesting which takes place after we moved to Wisconsin.

Patricia explains; "Then there is the story about when Dad needed help with bailing hay. Just to preface, this is what he gets for having a bunch of girls first before any boys arrived. Anyway, he puts me on the tractor with bailer behind. He and Nancy were on the wagon behind the bailer. He was stacking the bales, as they would come out. Well, we are going down hill in this one field and the tractor gets going too fast. I was trying to brake, but must have hit the clutch so he kept yelling 'let out the clutch.' Well, to a novice, what is the difference between the clutch and the brake? They both look the same! The rest of the story is nobody got hurt!" Because I am a farm wife I need to complete the above story. As the tractor started down the hill too fast when Pat pushed in the clutch it disengaged the engine which allowed the tractor to go even faster down the hill. She should have used the brake lightly; too hard and she would have killed the engine. All of this is a bit much for a detasseler driver. Her experience driving that machine didn't prepare her for baling on hills. There is more about this story to follow in Nancy's chapter. What was she doing on the wagon?

Patricia remained in Illinois when the family moved to Wisconsin because she was also going to Northern Illinois University. She was majoring in English and had plans to become an English teacher. That didn't work out because she decided to marry John Sauber who had gone to grade school with her in Virgil. Pat & John lived in Sycamore when they were first married but relocated to Caro, Michigan because of John's job. At the time of the move they had only Lisa who was just ready to go to kindergarten. Her only concern was whether there would be a kindergarten in Michigan for her to attend. Pat and John had three girls; Lisa Marie, Stephanie Lynn, and Kimberly Ann. Here is an interesting note about their names and how close Pat & I came to using the same names for our children. When I was thinking about names for my second child I knew if I had another girl I would use the name Stephanie or Kimberly. Because my Valerie's middle name is Lynn I thought it would be neat to have my second child with the same middle name. When Stephanie was born I couldn't believe my sister even used my chosen middle name. We had not discussed names for children and I wasn't pregnant at the time so I knew I would move on to Kimberly Lynn. In 1977 Pat and I were both expecting but her Kim was born three months before my second child and she used the only name I had left for a girl. Turns out when my Kevin was born I didn't need to be concerned with the girl's name that was no longer available but now I had to come up with a boy's name. Raymond and I decided on Kevin Ray. When I told Pat she explained that before Kim was born she had the name Kevin John picked out if she had a boy. See how nice things worked out for us.

Once John told me that he could see how little kids loved my Dad because of how friendly he always is. We were at some family celebration; maybe a wedding, and Dad was playing with a little child that was not willing to go back to his mother, which would cause anyone consternation. She was not pleased that the baby wanted to stay with Dad and I don't remember the woman's name. Her baby had found someone more interesting and she was crushed. Pat and John have remained friends after their divorce in 1985.

Currently, Pat works at the Tuscola County Courthouse in Caro, MI as a court recorder in Family/Probate Court. Her duties include scheduling hearings, recording hearings and preparing transcripts when they are needed. She does a lot of typing and has become very efficient. Because of Pat's job she comes in contact with many lawyers. I am sure it was with Pat's job in mind that Dad forwarded an e-mail that included the following. Even if you are not in contact with lawyers/attorneys, you can see the humor.

Attorney: Doctor, before you performed the autopsy, did you check for a pulse? Witness: No.

Attorney: Did you check for blood pressure? Witness: No.

Attorney: Did you check for breathing? Witness: No.

Attorney: So, then it is possible that the patient was alive when you began the autopsy? Witness: No.

Attorney: How can you be so sure, Doctor? Witness: Because his brain was sitting on my desk in a jar.

Attorney: I see, but could the patient have still been alive, nevertheless?

Witness: Yes, it is possible that he could have been alive and practicing law.

Dad will tell you that Pat's first-born child; Lisa was their first grandchild. He has recorded the birth dates of all of his grandchildren and a few of his great-grandchildren. I talked to Pat's three girls about what they remember of their Mother's parents. All of them love Wisconsin cheese curds, which were introduced to them by their Grandparents. Here are their stories.

Lisa is a high school chemistry teacher in Michigan. Her favorite story about Dad is how they always ate ice cream together when she was young. He would put a spoon in his pocket and tell her to follow him down the basement. He would take the large container of ice cream out of the freezer and sit her on top of the freezer. Then they would eat until they were full. I asked if she meant he took two spoons; "no, only one," was her reply. Now Lisa has two children; Braydon and Josilyn.

Stephanie works in media advertising in Central Michigan. While talking to her about advertising I explained I do most of the advertising for our bank. With all the money I spend for the bank I still believe word of mouth is the best type of advertising. The only cost with word of mouth is good customer service. Stephanie's story confirms the idea that young children should not watch TV before the age of three because they are still forming their reality. She explained that once when she was visiting Mom and Dad at the second farm in Loyal where they lived; she saw a show on Ripley's Believe It Or Not about haunted houses. After that she was sure her grandparents' home was full of ghosts. The new home Mom and Dad built a few years later didn't present a problem for her. She is married to Shawn Snell and they have one son, Quentin.

Kimberly remembers when Mom sold Avon. Kim explained that Mom was always generous with the tiny lipstick samples from her Avon kit. Grandma demonstrated to her how easy it was to follow her lip line. Kim understood she needed to stay inside the line Mom drew with a lip liner. She also told me about the carrot story, which will be a part of our family folklore for a few more generations. This story begins with Dad making a trip to Michigan to visit Pat's home. Because he doesn't get there often it was planned that he visit each of the girls and have a meal with them. It isn't important but Pat told me later that they should have done a better job of planning or coordinating the meals because all three of her daughters served chicken. Dad would never complain. When they were at Kim's, she served cooked baby carrots. As her son Nathan was trying to cut a carrot it flew off his plate. He was looking for it when Grandpa showed him that it had landed in Grandpa's sleeve. Nathan never tires of telling that story.

My sister Patricia and I have walked the Mackinac Bridge for the last 4 years. While cleaning out my mother's things, I found information about the bridge walk; which takes place every Labor Day. I talked to Pat about the walk and she had done it once with friends about 4 years earlier. When she did it the first time must have been when Mom got the information. The bridge is closed to drivers going east on Labor Day. At 7AM the Governor of the Michigan flies in using a helicopter and starts the 5-mile walk. Actually, if you want to run across you can start at that time. Walkers use the two east lanes of the bridge until 9:30 AM; while the two west lanes are used for vehicular traffic. After 9:30 AM only one east lane is available to walkers. If you are a walker, you can start anytime up until 11AM that day. Pat saw the Governor's helicopter the first year. But now that we walk it every year, our tradition is have breakfast at 7AM and then head for the bridge. The first 2 years we were alone but the last 2 years our significant others have joined us. One of these years we want to try to have children and/or grandchildren walk with us.

Pat also will forward things she has found on the Internet. One of my favorites about accepting what has happen to you in life follows:

A king, who did not believe in the goodness of God, had a slave who, in all circumstances, would always say "my king, do not be discouraged, because everything God does is perfect. He makes no mistakes!" One day they went hunting and along the way a wild animal attacked the king. His slave managed to kill the animal, but could not prevent his majesty from losing a finger. Furious and without showing his gratitude for being saved, the nobleman asked, "Is God good? If He was good, I would not have been attacked and lost my finger." The slave replied, "My king, despite all these things, I can only tell you that God is good, and he knows why these things happened. What God does is perfect. He is never wrong!" Outraged by the response, the king ordered the arrest of his slave. Later, the King left for another hunt, this time alone. Savages who engaged in human sacrifices captured him. On the altar and ready to sacrifice the nobleman, the savages discovered that their victim did not have one of his fingers. According to them, only a whole person with all his/her parts intact could be offered to the gods. The King without a finger was deemed an abominable sacrifice for their gods. So they released the King. Upon his return to the palace, the King authorized the release of his slave. He received the slave affectionately. He said to his slave, "God was really good to me! I was almost killed by the wild men, but for lack of a single finger, I was let go! But I have a question: if God is so good, why did he allow me to put you in jail?" The slave answered, "My King, if I had gone with you on this hunt, I would have been sacrificed instead because I have no missing finger. Remember everything God does is perfect. He is never wrong. He made you keep me in jail so I would not be with you on the hunt." Often we complain about life, and negative things that happen to us, forgetting that nothing is random and that everything has a purpose. Every morning, offer your day to God, don't be in a rush. Ask God to inspire your thoughts, guide your actions, and ease your feelings. And do not be afraid. God is never wrong!

She also posts on Facebook, one of her best was "no matter what life throws at me, at least I don't have ugly children." Her sense of humor is boundless.

5/ Too Blessed To Be Stressed

When I asked for a current picture of each of our families I knew we needed to have two for Pam's family. My sister, Pam is in the middle. Starting with Jenny on the left at 9 o'clock and moving clockwise; Randy, John, Patrick, Kurt, Jodi, Peggy, and Kris.

Grandchildren: In a perfect world this picture would be centered so we could see the "Meyer Farm" logo and Jodi's Addison would be pictured but she was born a year after this picture was taken. Front row, left to right: Kurt's Brittany holding Kurt's Kortney, Kris's Ty, Kurt's Sydney, Kurt's Gage, John's Alexis, & John's Jackson. Back row: Jenny's Kaylee, Jenny's Tragen, Kurt's Kolt held by Jenny's Amanda, & Peggy's Kyle holding Kurt's Wyat.

Pamela is the third child and she is a skilled seamstress. This is a talent of our mother's that was passed down to some of her children. Mom did a lot of sewing and mending as well as knitting and crocheting. Pam has raised seven children and now has 14 grandchildren with four of her children married. There is no end to her energy, she just recently retired from working full-time with her business, Fun Fitness in Loyal. Her days and many evenings are now filled with watching her grandchildren at their sporting and school events. Remember back in chapter one I mentioned about the audacity of this sister Pam after hearing my Dad's favorite story about her? Dad thinks Pam was about 5 or 6 years old when she told him, "I think you should have had only one child and it should have been me." Without stating the obvious, Dad laughs as he remembers Pamela making this statement. He explained she was sitting in the back seat and he has no idea what prompted her to make the statement. He does recall they were waiting for Mom. Really Pam? She doesn't remember the situation but I do know the car would be crowded with the whole family going someplace together. Once I could drive there were times we went to family gathering in two vehicles.

I do remember that Pam was a quiet, reflective child. Now as an adult, little has changed. When she makes a suggestion about whatever is being decided, take time to listen to her. When her ideas are considered she usually has come up with the solution. I'm thinking of the family get-togethers that we have when the Minnesota and Michigan sisters come to Loyal. Pam can come up with some great ideas from a cookie exchange to Munson Bridge Winery for wine tasting. Commercial break: This winery offers a wide variety of fruit wines with my favorite being their raspberry chocolate wine. This was where we learned that to win awards for making wine you have to produce a dry wine. But if you want to sell wine you need to produce the sweeter wines. Munson does work on both; winning awards and selling wine. But it is true; I do buy and enjoy the sweeter wine. A true wine connoisseur would say I have an immature palate, that would be an opinion not actual fact.

Back to Pam's family, she didn't raise those kids all by herself; she had help from her husband Randall Meyer. She met this guy in high school so I guess Loyal was an OK place to attend school. Back in 1968 when we moved from Illinois Pam had completed one year of high school at Kaneland. That first year after we moved, she wrote to a few friends and received letters in the mail from them. If not for that move she might not have found Mr. Right. Randy started farming when he graduated from high school. He went into partnership with his parents. Randy and Pam eventually took over his parents' dairy farm and milk anywhere up to 200 cows three times a day. Randy was active in FFA (Future Farmers of America) while in high school and received the American Farmer Degree. For about 10 years Pam did the midnight milking. I remember we were headed to Michigan to visit our sister Patricia and we had stopped about 10 PM to sleep at a motel. Pam made the comment that she might not be able to sleep because she was usually getting up to milk about that time of night. We did OK getting a good night's sleep and in the morning made our way to Caro, MI.

Pamela wrote her own stories about our parents and they are as follows:

"One of my favorite memories with Dad was flying. It was always great going up in the big blue sky; through the clouds and over the land around our farm, which gave me an opportunity to see so much from the air. We had our own landing strip or small airport. Dad would check the weather and the direction of the wind. If it was OK up and away we would go. I remember once flying to a farm show in Peoria, Illinois. Harold Engel and his daughter Susie went with us. This would have been when Dad had his 4-seater plane. We had a great time but on the way home we did hit some turbulence. That was not good on the stomachs but we made it home and were happy to see our landing strip and hanger. It was also always fun to ride with Dad on his milk route. Dad had two semi-trucks with bulk milk trailers. We would pick up milk and go to Modern Dairy, the factory in Elgin. There we would look for Irvin Roush who was called Shag. The reason we wanted to find Shag was because he always gave me a carton of chocolate milk. There was a few times on the route that you remained in the truck because the farmer had a big dog that Dad didn't trust not to bite. That was Dad always looking out for what was best for me."

Pam continues her story; "Mom is the reason I read so much. She ordered my first series of books, <u>The Happy Hollisters</u>. Every month a book would come and I would get it done and be ready for the next one in less than 30 days. I always wished for more books than one a month. I also got a magazine in the mail but the books were by far the best. Mom helped me with my first quilt. We were living in Wisconsin so I would have been in high school. I sewed the 8 X 8 squares together and then we set up the quilting frame in the living room. It was just about wall-to-wall when the frame was set up to use. So around we would go tying the layers together. Sometimes someone would be underneath ready to send the needle and yarn back up to be tied. I still love to quilt today all thanks to Mom."

There is an official web site for <u>The Happy Hollisters</u>, which were published in the 1950's and 1960's. It was a mystery series with 33 titles written by Jerry West, the pen name used by Andrew Svenson. The books my sister read were no longer published but have been re-printed because Grandparents wanted to share them with their Grandchildren. The children in the stories are based on the author's own children. I found the history of how the family received the royalties to the books interesting. After the author's death the company that had been publishing them during his life gave all rights for The Happy Hollisters to his wife. I don't think something like that would happen today because of what I would call "corporate greed." Maybe I am wrong, but it is a nice to know the family controls the rights to the books.

Now let us move on to Pam's own children. She could write her own stories about her crew but I had fun interviewing all of them. Instead of starting with Pam and Randy's oldest child and working my way to the youngest, I'll go in reverse and see if I get them all in this chapter. So we start with the baby, Kris who is 25 years old and living closer to me than his mother. He lives in Junction City about 5 miles from me; that's why he calls me neighbor. Pam is lucky to have all her kids living within the state of Wisconsin. Kris is a herdsman and supervises the milking of 120 registered cows with an expansion planned for 2014. At some point there will be 1100 registered animals to keep him busy. Makes me tired just thinking about how hard he must work. This year when Ray was ready to sell his corn he checked with Kris to see if they would be interested in purchasing our corn and taking it off the field. They came in with the big machinery that farmers have now days; Ray's 43 acres were off in six hours. The reason it took that long was because Kris held the trucks up as he changed silos. Kris, my neighbor; has one son Ty; who is 9 years old. He will spell his name for you when he meets you for the first time. "T Y, my name is short and easy to spell." Can't argue with the little guy.

Kurt is next; he and his wife Lori have six children. Brittney, Sidney, Gage, Kolt, Wyatt, and Kortney who range in age from 1 to 8 years. Do you see a pattern here; another busy and hard working family? Kurt works in Dorchester for Meyer Manufacturing; they make farm machinery. Their web site says, "Farm equipment buyers trust the name Meyer." That is true, you can trust the Meyer name, but Kurt isn't working for relatives. Grandma Pam told me about 4 year old Kolt who came to the rescue of his 7 year old sister Sidney, who was in second grade during the 2013-14 school year. When school started that September, apparently there was another second grader picking on Sidney. Little Kolt told the boy to leave his sister alone. The kid told Kolt to just hit him. Kolt gave him one in the nose. I can hear Kurt explaining to his son that hitting others is not acceptable. Pam doesn't know if Kolt actually got in trouble at school but this is one of those family stories that could grow into family folklore, as it is re-told during the coming years.

"John is John." What else is there to say about the next boy? But I will try to explain what is meant by that phrase. When Maria and John got married she designed a very neat, simple program for the wedding service. Apparently she didn't get any input from John most likely because she knows, "John is John." At the rehearsal when there was a break in the action the priest complimented John on the beautiful program. "Pardon me, the what?" was John's reply. See John is John and if Maria is happy, John is happy. She just knows him well enough not to concern him with certain issues. They have two children, Alexis and Jackson. John also works as a herdsman and does field work on his Uncle Larry's farm. He lives less than a mile from his parent's farm.

When Patrick was to celebrate his 35th birthday, he wanted to do something with friends. There was a half-barrel set up in Greenwood one Saturday night in June 2012. Patrick was missing in action, meaning he had two places to be the night of his party. He was a sub on a softball team and the tournament was going just a bit too long which was the reason he didn't get to the party on time. When he finally did arrive there was a row of "birthday" shots lined up on the bar for him. He asked himself, "What would Grandpa do?" So he drank them down. I know there is more to this story but I didn't ask. Patrick has a degree in Physical Education from University of Wisconsin-River Falls. He was doing some substitute teaching but has opted to work at Meyer Manufacturing to have full-time steady employment. He accepted a coaching position at University of Wisconsin-Marshfield as the head basketball coach. I love to watch basketball so I enjoyed hearing about his success and look forward to seeing my Godchild coach the Marauders for many winters to come. Might make the Wisconsin winter enjoyable; that is a bit of a stretch.

Jodi studied to be an agriculture teacher and was at Stevens Point Area Senior High or SPASH for more than 10 years. This was the high school that my children attended but they had graduated by the time she started teaching. Because her job at SPASH was cut to part time for a few years she traveled between the high school and the two junior highs to teach her classes. To earn some extra money she opened her own embroidering and printing business. She could design team t-shirts and any other item of clothing you wanted. In 2013-14 she took a full time teaching position at Hillsboro School District. She teaches a wide variety of classes: some of which were new to her, but she never backs away from a challenge. She teaches both basic and advanced Ag mechanics. Other classes include animal science, food science, Ag processing, 7th and 8th grade exploratory which introduces the students to her class offerings. She and Johnny have Addison Jo; who was one year old in 2014, to add to her workload. She can handle it because she comes from a hard working family.

Peggy works in Marshfield as a dental hygienist. She and Paul have one son, Kyle. He is at the age where he is ready to drive. Can you remember the days when you had to let your kids take the car out on the road? Strikes terror in a parent's heart but Kyle is dependable so it should all be good. Kyle is a sophomore at Marshfield Senior High where I was a teacher. I missed having him as a student by about 10 years. Kyle participates in football, basketball, and baseball. Peggy told me about a time she was looking for some advice from Grandpa. He told her to just make a decision and stick with the consequences. That sounds like good advice that we can all use in our daily lives.

In the Bible it says something like the "last shall be first and the first shall be last." Thus we come to Jennifer who is Pam's first born. She and Chad Bogdonovich have three children. They are Kaylee, Tragen, and Amanda. Before Kaylee drove, Grandpa took Jennifer's kids to school in the morning. They live in the Loyal school district but have elected to go to Greenwood and there isn't a bus that can get them to school. Grandpa has a van with a DVD player, so the 15-minute trip went fast when they were watching a movie. When Grandpa (actually this is their Great-Grandpa) got the new van he had a Lone Ranger movie for them to watch the first day. It has been said, they had a movie of their own to watch the next day, guess they weren't interested in a black and white film. When the DVD was turned off it stayed in the same place for them and they could start watching again when they got back in the van. Kaylee doesn't have a van with a DVD player; guess they went back to watching movies at home. Another thing they miss with Kaylee taking them to school is an adult signature. Every once in a while they needed an adult to look at their homework and sign it. Grandpa would take care of signing paperwork for them a few times during the years he drove them to school. Why did this happen? Because sometimes kids don't look at their homework until it is time to go to school the next day. This leads us to the next story.

Pam was hemming a dress for Kaylee for homecoming at the last minute in the fall of 2013. Why it was last minute was my only question. When Kaylee decided she needed a dress for homecoming Pam suggested shortening the dress from the spring prom. Kaylee said she would think about it and she decided that was a good idea. Pam also suggested adding a different accent color so it would look like a completely new dress. Pam knew the homecoming was getting close and wondered if Kaylee had changed her mind because no one brought the dress to her for the alterations. When she mentioned the situation to Randy he just laughed because the dress had been in Amanda's backpack for about a week. When Pam talked to Amanda is when she finally got the dress with only a day remaining to get it ready on time. It was completed for Kaylee to the attend homecoming dance. Pam works well under pressure while that is not a trait I share with my younger sister.

"Each one should test his own actions. Then he can take pride in himself, without comparing himself to somebody else." Galatians 6:4. I used this Bible verse because it describes how this family does compete with each other. They showed dairy cattle for several years. My kids showed for 4-H but

Pam's kids also showed with FFA. When my kids were showing cattle that was the only way I was involved with our dairy farm. I helped train, groom, and get everybody to the fair on time. I only had two but Pam had all of her kids showing at one point. The Meyer family no longer shows dairy cattle; but has moved on to showing horses. As an observation on my part, it is as time consuming as showing cattle. The one difference I have noticed is in dairy the person leading the animal is in all white. What color would you not want your child to be in when working with cattle? White would be my replay. But when showing horses the person involved is actually in their Sunday best, with a western look. Not that their clothes stay any cleaner; but, a dark color might hide a small stain.

Showing horses is a hobby the entire family can enjoy together. Randy shows his Belgian horses at many local fairs and has the pyramid hitch at Farm Technology Days. Jenny, Jodi, Patrick and Kris helped him at Barron, Wisconsin where Technology Days were held in 2013. That event moves around the state each year and in 2014 it will be close to me in Stevens Point. John and Kurt also own horses and show with their families at county fairs. They enjoy the competition and once in a while the kids are able to beat their Dad. Keep in mind Randy has taught them everything they know about horses. It makes for a good story when the youngsters win a few ribbons. Peggy is the only one in the family that doesn't own or show horses but she does join in the fun. She is the official photographer for the Pam-A-Rand farm and she does do a great job.

Kyle and Kaylee have been showing for 7 years. In 2013) Kyle took first place in showmanship at the Marshfield Fair.

Tragen has been showing for 4 years and won the trophy for high points at that fair in the 11 to 13 year old division. He won the same trophy two years ago for 8 to 10 year olds. Amanda has been showing for 3 years and won the high point trophy in that same age group last year. Kaylee has also won that award for 14 to 17 year olds. Ty and Brittney showed for the first time this year and both came away with first place ribbons at different fairs. I hope these two know that starting at the top only gives you one way to go, but then you can strive to stay at the top. They were both pleased with their results. Grandpa and Grandma are pleased that their children as well as their grandchildren have been successful with this family hobby.

Just considering the technology that Pam's grandchildren now have makes me remember the limited resources we had. While talking to my sisters and brothers about what to put in this book I was telling them I can remember getting our first TV. They think I am making this up and after talking to Dad I guess I don't remember the first family TV because Dad said they had one before I was born. I only remember watching TV in Maple Park; which is the fourth family home, but we lived there for more than 12 years. I had started kindergarten in Elburn but moved to Maple Park. Dad thinks we moved sometime in early March but I only remember the teacher in Maple Park. Her name was Mrs. Anderson and her only son was in our class. No one can remember not having a telephone when we were in Illinois but it was hooked to a wall and we never lost the phone. Now Pam's kids all have a phone hooked to their belts or in their purses. These phones can take pictures, tell time, and have so many aps (applications) who knows what else their phones can do.

The Friday after Thanksgiving was a day of shopping for my sister Pam and I when our children were younger. She was shopping for seven while I only had two to get ready for Christmas. That tradition has gone by the wayside because we no longer have to get the "latest thing" that is out for Christmas. Money works; it is always the right color and size and does not need to be dusted. My money talks, it says goodbye. Actually now on Thanksgiving Day Raymond, Valerie, and I do a 5-K walk in Marshfield sponsored by Festival Foods. You get a t-shirt and pumpkin pie with your entry fee. There is an opportunity for us to donate the pie to a local food pantry. Our pies go there because when we go to Pam's for Thanksgiving dinner and there is always plenty of dessert after too much turkey.

Pam's family does help Grandpa out a lot because he lives so close to them in Loyal. There was a time when any spring, Grandpa could go to the farm and get a tractor job. Some of those big tractors were hard for Grandpa to get in but the boys made steps to help him. Patrick lives just three houses down from Dad in Loyal, which makes it nice, knowing someone is close to Dad. There have been times when it has snowed and Pam's family was there to plow Grandpa out before he could get out and do it himself. Dad does have an 18-horse tractor to mow the lawn with and during the winter he has a snow blower for it. He likes blowing snow and even drives around Loyal to help others with their driveway. Pam has always been there for both Mom and Dad when they have needed help.

6/Growing old is mandatory; growing up is optional

Had to use an old picture of Ralph. This was taken in Maple Park for my First Communion in 1956. Ralph is the baby in the picture. Left to right: Pamela, Grandma Helen Eder holding JR, Connie, Grandpa Anton Eder. Patricia is in front.

Ralph JR is the first-born son of my parents. He is referred to as Ralph, or Ralph JR; but never Pat. Mom mentioned once that Dad was more mature after the birth of his first son.

Don't know if everyone would agree with that assessment but that is what she believed. Ralph has one child, Zachary who lives next to our Dad in Loyal, Wisconsin. Zachary and his wife Amy have two children; Hunter and Katie. JR loves his Harley and enjoys riding with friends. When I asked for a picture of him with his family I suggested to him that everybody stand behind the Harley. Is it really necessary to capitalize Harley? Anyway I saw Katie riding a little battery operated 4-wheeler and mentioned it would be cute with her sitting on that in front. Ralph asked with alarm, "With the Harley?" Guess that was a poor suggestion on my part, because I didn't take the picture when everyone was together because we didn't have the Harley so that picture didn't happen.

Ralph JR's favorite story about Dad has to be the "grease" story. JR must have been about 7 years old and he had 6-year old Nancy as a sidekick when they got in trouble. According to "family folk lore" we didn't know about the trouble they had gotten into until we found the evidence two years later. Dad was a CenPeCo distributor in the Maple Park area. Orders were taken by the company and sent to area distributors for delivery. In the spring of 1963 Dad got a shipment of grease & oil he needed to deliver. As he was taking inventory and getting ready to deliver the products he found he was a case short of grease cartridges. The man that delivered the inventory to our place explained he felt that the order was complete but he supplied an extra 24 grease cartridges for Dad because Dad could not find them. Dad had a trailer that he used to store the grease and oil in until he was able to get it all delivered. One case was truly missing and he didn't find out "the rest of the story" (to quote Paul Harvey) until two years later when he moved tht trailer. JR and Nancy took the case of grease cartridges under the trailer and smashed them and used the grease as paint. If you ask Ralph about what he was thinking at the time he'll explain that it was fun to see the cartridges pop open when hit against something solid. Nancy says she was just following her older brother's example. When Dad found the mess he said it looked like they had some fun for a while.

Dad told me about how mechanical little Ralph JR was when we were still living in Illinois. This happened when Ralph was about 8 or 9 years old. Once when Dad arrived home from the milk route, JR greeted him with a flat tire off the lawn mower. We were going to mow the lawn but the mower had a flat tire. Ralph took it off so Dad could fix it when he got home from work. Too bad the wheel was cast iron and he had used a hammer or maul to "break" it off. Dad said he couldn't yell at the little guy, he was so proud of himself. My parents must have been made of patience.

Once when JR flew with Dad and Nancy to a farm show all was going well until they landed. At that point they wanted JR to cross a swinging bridge. He had just been in a plane with Dad and now there was a bridge in his way. The bridge took the people that had flown in across to the main displays of farm machinery. Dad expressed the concern that he didn't think Ralph was going across that bridge. After everyone relaxed and they watched others go across JR said it was OK and he was able to cross the bridge. No one mentioned the return trip so it must have been easier to cross the bridge the second time. This story just explains how patient our Dad could be; they would have gone home without seeing the show if Ralph had decided he could not cross that bridge. In Yosemite Valley there is a popular destination with a swinging bridge that offers an excellent view of Yosemite Falls. My thought is that JR would not be interested and wouldn't consider making that trip to see the Falls.

Apparently Nancy listened to what ever her big brother told her. Dad remembers a time the two of them were making baking powder biscuits. After JR put the baking powder in his batter there wasn't enough for Nancy's batch. JR told her she didn't need that stuff. When the two batches of biscuits were baked it was obvious she had been led astray. His biscuits were good while hers were like rocks. Yes, of course, they had to play catch with Nancy's biscuits and I think JR even tried to kick a few over the shed; but then that might be one of those embellished stories that grow into folklore over time.

For the sake of this next story, I'm going to say this event took place the Christmas of 1964. We were opening our Christmas presents on Christmas Eve. I do believe Santa delivered the gifts because Al would have been two years old. Mom wanted us to open the gifts one-at-a-time so we could see what everyone got. It didn't always work that way but I did see the truck that JR unwrapped that year. He told Mom that he had seen one just like this one in the basement. What? Too late kid; he had just confessed to snooping for Christmas presents.

Ralph JR's favorite story about Mom was when we left Maple Park for the last time and moved to Granton, Wisconsin. Mom was driving a 1956 Chevy station wagon with the two boys while I was following in a car with the girls. We didn't go a mile from home before we had to stop because Mom needed to rescue a cat from Laddie, Ralph's dog. The dog had decided to chase the poor cat. Mom had plants in that station wagon so that provided cover for the cat but she had to separate the two animals. That trip should have taken us about 4 hours but once Al realized that the blue signs along the toll way meant there was a bathroom for him to use, he needed to stop at every one of those waysides. Because he saw all the blue signs that 4 hour trip took us more than eight hours. Dad said another time little Al tried to pull that trick on him. They had stopped for Al to go to the bathroom and about an hour later Al said he needed to stop again. Dad told him no. "You want me to wet my pants?" Al asked. Dad just shrugged his shoulders and Al didn't wet his pants. It never took Dad 8 hours to make that trip with or without Albert.

Dad, Patricia, and I were talking about the length of time for that drive from Illinois to Wisconsin. Pat felt that it was more like a 5-hour trip instead of my calculation of 4 hours. She and I drive home from college for a few years after our family moved to Loyal. Dad asked if I remembered the time he and I drove it in three hours; I did remember but I forgot the reason. Apparently we already owned the farm in Wisconsin. A neighbor, Fritz Boldt, was milking the cows that were in the barn. Fritz called Dad and said he had found a herd of cows that would be excellent to add to our herd. At issue was the money; it was needed sooner instead of later. Dad and I made a quick trip to Wisconsin with cash, no checks allowed. "No checks" set the stage for the quick 3-hour trip to the farm. Today it would still be a good idea not to take a check from someone you don't know but wiring money is an option. Check with your personal banker but keep in mind, cash is always king.

The farm where we moved, had a Granton address but was in the Loyal school district. When Mom had a phone put in the barn we didn't use it to call the house because it was long distance to call between the barn and the house. Dad used the barn phone to call the veterinarian or make other calls that farmers need to make. When we moved to Loyal Ralph JR was 10 or 11 years old. I am sure he helped Dad on the farm because he did eventually help Dad do the milking. He didn't remember the phone calls being long distance but he never was one to hang on the phone.

For this next story I need to give you some background. I was never the type of kid to tattle on my siblings. Think of me as a good person or the actual story might be that my brothers and sisters never got into trouble. You can believe what you want but just remember, I'm not a tattler. And for the rest of this story; it starts when we were sitting around talking about when we were younger, what we would like to have changed, and what decisions we would not change. "We" in this case was Mom, Dad, and maybe all my sisters. I know Ralph JR was not with us. I just asked, "Do you have a friend you would trust to take your clothes to the other end of town while you 'streaked' through town?" When Mom asked, "What is streaking and why would you ask such a question?" I knew I started down a path that was not going to end well. I had assumed my parents knew all about JR streaking through Loyal one year during a Corn Festival. This happened when he was in high school so it took place before June of 1974. My little story was news to them, up to that point this child had been a little angel or they were under that impression or was that an illusion? So as the story goes; my brother's friend, Keith Johnson was the person he and a few others trusted to be on the other end of town when they came streaking through town. You do know what streaking is, right? We explained it to Mom as "strip and run." That does just about cover the definition of the social phenomenon of the early 70's.

Once Ralph matured and graduated from high school he became the responsible adult he is today. After high school he worked in the cheese factory where he had a part-time job during his high school years. After graduation he even drove a milk truck for a few years. JR took over the farm in 1979 and Dad went to work as a field man for a Dairy plant. When I asked Dad how many cows Ralph JR milked when he took the farm over Dad's reply was, "all of them." What a sense of humor, but that didn't give me the information I was seeking. I had to turn to Zachary who told me his father milked 50 to 60 cows on the farm. My brother only farmed for about 10 years. He decided to sell in 1998 and work off the farm. The issue when working for yourself is health insurance. When you work out you can get into their insurance plan if offered. In my personal opinion it is always easier to work for someone else instead of owning your own business. Ralph went to work for Cummins Filtration in Neillsville in 1998 and has been there ever since. His son started two years later and also continues there today. This company started in 1958 known as the Seymour Filter Company. Their web site says it started with two employees and has grown to 5,500 employees. Today, the company is the world leader in filtration and exhaust products for heavy-duty diesel engines.

A few years ago Ray and I went with Dad, JR, and Zachary to a dairy breakfast. In Wisconsin June is dairy month and if you own a farm you can sponsor a dairy breakfast. By attending a dairy breakfast you can learn all sorts of interesting trivia facts about Wisconsin and the dairy industry. Did you know that it takes more cows to produce milk annually for Pizza Hut (about 170,000) than there are people in Green Bay, Wisconsin? Or, did you know that the average cow produces enough milk each day to fill six one-gallon jugs, which means it is about 55 pounds of milk? This is where I learned that cows have an acute sense of smell and can smell something up to six miles away. So those cows are aware of the "barn smell." Enough facts? If not just google fun facts or trivia about June dairy month in Wisconsin; there are many sites. While we were waiting in line to get our breakfast I took a three-generation picture of those three. Dad is about 5 feet 6 inches; JR is about 3 inches taller and Zachary has them both beat at 6 feet. One last thing about a dairy breakfast in Wisconsin: it is the one time ice cream is served in the morning. And it takes 12 pounds of whole milk to make one gallon of ice cream.

Earlier I had mentioned that Zachary and his family live next to Dad in town. Once this summer; when I was visiting Dad, Zack came over to get Dad's riding mower. It is a John Deere tractor. The John Deere green makes it either high quality or expensive. It is a really nice riding lawn mower. Zachary proceeded to mow his lawn as well as Dad's. When winter comes he and JR will take off the mower deck and put on the snowplow. Dad likes to push snow in the winter. It is not an unusual site to see him driving his tractor with the blower on the front down a street in Loyal. He heads around town to help people, mostly ladies, with their snow removal. This might be the reason some have referred to Dad as a "ladies' man." The story behind that title comes from Amy. As it was told to me, Loyal was doing some kind of upgrade to their water system. Each family was to have their water tested and there was a person going door to door by appointment to get the job done. The man had been at Amy's and he was to go to Dad's but he was a half an hour early for that appointment. Amy offered to help the guy out and called to see if Dad was available, he was and told Amy to send him over. After Dad's water was tested, Dad asked if he had been to Patrick's place. Patrick is the grandson of Dad's that lives four houses from him. The guy told him he had not been able to set up an appointment with Patrick because no one was home. Dad explained he could get him in because that was his grandson and Dad knew Patrick was at work. While at Patrick's place Dad and this man were talking. The guy told Dad that Amy had said Dad was quite a "ladies' man." That Amy really knows my Father. Back to this "ladies' man" deal: Dad just likes to help people and there seems to be more women than men that need help. Dad has coffee every morning with his friend Diane Phillips who lives about six blocks from him. She went with him to visit a friend in Reedsburg, Arlene Engle who lost her husband, Harold a few years ago. Harold and Arlene had been friends of Mom and Dad's when we lived in Illinois. Engle's also moved to Wisconsin to purchase a farm.

Zachary's wife Amy has a big garden in their back yard. After harvesting from her vegetable garden she prepares the vegetables and does some canning. She also makes jam and wine from grapes and cherries. She told Dad that she wasn't sure why she was making the wine because she doesn't drink or like wine. Don't worry about it Dad told her, "Just bring it over when it is ready." She also is making some brandy, which sounds like a lot of work because it won't be ready for a year. Patience is what that takes.

CM Mary

In May, 2013 when our sister Patricia made the trip to Wisconsin for a visit we made plans to go to church on Saturday night in Willard. The 4 PM Mass worked great at Holy Family Catholic Church. Because our brother Ralph lives in Willard we could visit with him and have supper after Mass. It was decided we would meet at the local bar, Freddie's Pub just a block from where we attended Mass. We rode together to church in Pat's car. Now lets follow her line of thinking as she closed and locked her car door; put the keys in my purse, take money out for the collection, I don't need to take my purse into church. Yep that was where she stopped thinking and closed the car door. What she said before she took a step away from the car was not a phrase a person should use just before going into the house of God to pray. OK, let's call somebody. Can't do that, all the cell phones are locked safely in the car, except Dad's. We did catch a lucky break and called John to see if he could come and have the car unlocked while we were in church. John is a mechanic that lives in Loyal who works on Dad's vehicles. Dad's cell phone wasn't on but that is typical for him. We turned it on and made the call, John would be our savior. As we went into church you would think we would turn the phone off but we didn't. Good part of this story I did think of it before someone tried to call Dad. After communion I checked to see if John had arrived and found him working to unlock the car without much luck. When we got out of church we were hopeful that he could open it but it just wasn't meant to be. He took Dad home to get his van because it wasn't looking good as far as getting that car open. JR was at Freddie's, only a block away and couldn't figure out why we weren't coming to meet him. I guess Dad called him to say unless we decided to walk the block to the bar he would find us camped out in front of the vehicle in the church parking lot. JR drove down to lend support, which didn't open the car, but he had a cell phone. He also had many suggestions for Patricia: like keep a key under your hood, or in your wallet. Her wallet was in the car along with the keys; see women don't carry their wallets in their back pockets. Do you have any other ideas, genius? Pat decided to call AAA. That guy came to our rescue and we were finally were able to go to supper using Pat's car.

Did you know that the acronym NASCAR stands for National Association for Stock Car Auto Racing? Ralph and Nancy are both really into this racing thing and I bet neither one of them know what the acronym means. I didn't realize it wasn't a word. What I mean is they both enjoy watching NASCAR, not actually driving the cars. Here is another activity where Nancy follows her big brother's lead. While her favorite driver is #99, Carl Edwards; Ralph JR's favorite NASCAR driver is Kevin Harvick, #29. His number is going to change next year and I have no idea what his new number will be. When my brother went to Bristol Motor Speedway in Tennessee I know Nancy was disappointed she couldn't go with him. When JR and his friends go to the race, they rent a place that offers them a ride to and from the race. They are dropped off right at the front entrance. Now that is real service. My son Kevin lived in Kingsport, TN, which is 20 minutes from Bristol. People that live in the area never venture close to Bristol when there is a NASCAR race; the seating capacity of the stadium is 165,000. I have been to the Speedway but not on a race day. After Thanksgiving downhill sledding is offered for the public. Tennessee doesn't get a lot of snow but then they don't need snow. On one of the hills in the parking lot heavy plastic sheets or mats are placed on the ground. Then we were given an inner tube to slide down the hill; if you wanted to go faster they would spray the bottom of your tube with water. Kevin with his two sons, Andrew and Parker and I went for an hour. One boy had to ride with either Kevin or myself. They both wanted to ride with Kevin because he always won the race to the bottom of the hill. He was heavier and he used the water. I didn't even enjoy racing down the hill; it went fast enough for me even without the water to reduce friction.

7/ But Where Are the Pictures?

Left to right: The Guy or Jim, Christy, Nancy, and Jerry.

Nancy was born only 18 months after JR. When they were growing up they played together and I guess got into trouble together. According to Nancy she was the follower and only doing what ever Ralph JR suggested. This is an interesting fact that JR does not deny. Nancy has two children; Christy and James. They are from her first marriage to James Milz, my husband's younger brother. When Nancy announced her engagement to Jim my Dad made the comment that one Milz in the Schmitt family was enough. My husband, not missing a beat, said it works both ways; one Schmitt in the Milz family was plenty. This is not the first time in our family's history that two sisters married two brothers. Dad's mother had a sister Rose who married Dad's father's brother, Albert.

Nancy was expecting their second child when her husband Jim died a month before Jimmy was born. Nancy was fortunate to meet and marry Jerry Locknane; he is a really great guy and if you heard Jerry talk about Nancy's children you would think they were his. Jerry is from Loyal but Nancy and Jerry's jobs moved them to Minnesota within 20 minutes of the Mall of America.

When going through our mother's things, Nancy was not pleased to find there are not a lot of pictures of her as a baby. It is a fact life that the oldest has an album and each child after that has fewer pictures to put in an album. Think about it, Nancy was number 5 and Mom was busy with laundry, cooking, baking, and sewing. Nancy was not neglected so I'm not sure less pictures is such a big deal. (Drama queen story to follow.) The bad part is that Albert, the next child, does have a nice album; but there is a good reason for that set of pictures. That album was a 4-H project for me. Pat and I took photography as a project and mine was making an album using the baby. Babies are always so cute and make for interesting subject matter. But keep in mind; we do have enough pictures of Nancy to know she was an adorable child.

Remember the baling story from Patricia's chapter? Nancy was on the wagon with Dad when they were speeding down the hill. She recalls "holding on for dear life." Those are her words; not mine. Using Pat's thoughts; "nobody got hurt."

And Dad doesn't remember it being all that bad. Ralph JR likes to say, "Nancy is a drama queen."

Mom told me about a tragedy that happened to a classmate of Nancy's during her junior year in high school. It would have been the summer of 1974. Nancy was in the house helping Mom when her boyfriend stopped by to ask her to go swimming. Mom told me that Nancy didn't want to go because it was actually a group of four boys, maybe if there had been another girl Nancy would have considered going. Her boyfriend's name was Mike Oestrick. Later in the afternoon his brother came back to our place to say that Mike had drown. The boys knew where he had gone down and after the rescue team was called they were able to retrieve the body. Nancy said she remembers Mom was out in the barn when they came to tell Nancy about the tragic event. So it was Mom that broke the news to her daughter. I remember Mom telling me that she was thankful Nancy had not been with because she might also have drowned. How sad for that Oestrick family.

Nancy graduated from Loyal Senior High in 1975. During her senior year she had the lead in the musical "Annie Get Your Gun." I can remember seeing that show on TV with Ethel Merman as the lead soloist. Merman could really belt out a song and my little sister Nancy did a wonderful job in that play. The story is a work of fiction based on the life of Annie Oakley and her romantic involvement with Frank Butler. Even today Nancy will sing as if no one is listening. She was telling us on her last birthday when she got to work early and cranked up the intercom to sing happy birthday to herself. One side note; she is the first one into the office most days so she knew no one was listening. Wouldn't it have been a surprise if her boss had a tape recorder set to keep a recording of all those announcements? Maybe he does have a recording of all announcements made; that would make life very interesting.

Another serious event; which took place during Nancy's senior year in high school, was on senior skip day. That skip day was a life-changing event in another family's life. There was another classmate that drown during that senior outing. The student had been pretending to be having trouble in the water a couple times during the day, when he actually had a problem and called for help no one came to his rescue. Again Nancy only heard about this after the fact. It was good she wasn't there because she had participated in the skip day and was out of school that day; the Lord keeping her safe yet one more time.

My Mom's funeral was the first one I ever had to help plan. For my sister Nancy it was the second because she had needed to plan Jim's. As we were working with the funeral director we realized these are the last decisions we would be making for our mother. For this reason we waited for Dad to tell us what he wanted and only helped him when he asked for our input. What to put on the funeral card was one of the things he wanted us to decide. Because Pat and Nancy were not with us at the funeral home we called their cell phones for their suggestions. They both reminded us that Mom always liked angels and the Prayer to Your Guardian Angel is the one prayer I remember Mom helping me to learn. I am sure she helped me with all my prayers but I remember her telling me that prayer was important to commit to memory and say everyday. It is one of the shortest prayers we needed to learn by heart. We used that prayer for her card along with the date of her birth and death. "Angel of God, my guardian dear, to whom God's love commits me here. Forever this day be at my side; to light, to guard, to rule, to guide."

After Jim's death Nancy moved to Iowa and then to Minnesota. This is the reason her two children did not graduate from the same high school. Nancy's first born; Christy graduated from West High School in Davenport, Iowa. She went on to study speech communications and has a master's degree in Ethics in Leadership from St Kate's University located in St. Paul, MN. For the fifteen years, she has worked in account management and sales roles in the talent assessment industry. Currently she is a Strategic Account Executive for CEB. She married Jason in 2007 and they are raising his two sons, Ryan and Austin.

Her favorite memory of Grandma is going to garage sales. Mom was never willing to pass one up. Christy can remember spending many afternoons sifting through other people's trash for treasures. Grandma always had interesting trinkets and knickknacks through out her house and Christy loved investigating the piles and digging in closets to see what she could find. Her favorite memory about Grandpa is what she referred to as "the infamous Spritz cookie fiasco!" I had never heard this family story. She explained the story. "Mom, Jim, Grandma, Grandpa and I were baking cookies for the holidays. Everybody was at one end of the counter mixing cookie batter and decorating except Grandpa. He was doing the food coloring at the other end. He decided it would be fun to mix all the colors together to see what would happen. Needless to say, the color was not good. They looked horrible." What Christy does remember is that if you closed your eyes, the taste was the same. It is a good thing that food coloring doesn't add a flavor.

Christy has written several books. I have a copy of her first book, <u>Edge of Shadows</u>. She uses the name Cege Smith as her pen name and has a website at www.cegesmith.com. If you enjoy paranormal stories, you will enjoy her books. I find it hard to keep up with reality but I enjoyed her character, Ellie Coulter in her first book. The plot is very involved when Ellie's ex-husband arrives on the scene to talk about dreams or premonitions he has about Ellie's death. The book does hold your attention to the end.

James (aka Jim), Nancy's second born graduated from Champlin High School Brooklyn Park MN; very close to where Nancy and Jerry now live. He has worked at AT&T since 2007 in the business customer service department. One of his favorite memories of Grandpa is when Grandpa picked him up in Davenport IA and they were on the way to Loyal for a visit. They were listening to an 8-track of some comedian and Grandpa was stopped for speeding. Jim would have only been about 10 years old at the time. Yet another family story I had never heard about if not for this book. See why I am writing this book? Jim remembers his Grandma as a creature of habit. She always had to watch Jeopardy and Wheel of Fortune. The other thing he remembered about watching those shows with Mom was that you didn't have to be quiet. A person could talk and ask a question about the show and that was OK with Mom. I mention this because in my home when the weather is on NO ONE is to talk. Guess the weather is important to a farmer, but even in the winter? Again I have to ask, really?

Now for Jim's "locked in" story: have you ever been trying to explain to a person how to get from point A to point B, and you could tell by the look on their face it just wasn't registering? According to family folklore, I'm "locked in now" means the directions finally make sense and we know how to get to point B. Who came up with that? The Guy. The story goes that 12 year old, Jimmy was suppose to be getting Grandpa and Patty around Maple Grove and he was getting them lost instead of to point B. Patricia explained that after a few turns, stops, & back ups Jimmy finally realized where they needed to go and how they needed to travel to get there. "I'm locked-in now" he told the adults depending on him.

Dad told me about another time Jim was riding with him. To explain, Jim never knew his father because he had died in June of 1981 while Jim was born in July of that year. He was close to his Grandpa for the first few years of his life and we were all concerned about Jim when they moved to Iowa. But back to Dad's story; he was taking Jim and Zachary someplace and they were in their seat belts in the back seat. Zachary is two years older than Jim and at the time of the story they might have been about 6 and 8 years old. Zachary was telling Jim that Grandpa was going to die sometime. Little Jim was telling him, no, that was not going to happen. Yes, Zachary was trying to explain, everybody has to die. So Jim had to ask Grandpa for his opinion. Grandpa explained to Jim that he wasn't going to die today. Guess that satisfied the little guy; because they went on to discuss something else. Another thing that we have to say about Jim was that he visited Mom & Dad in Texas on November 11, 2000. How do we know that? Because Mom would take the time to document different events in her life. When I was looking at her domino set of rules I found a notation that she, Dad, and Jim had played a game of dominos on 11/11/00. Mom and Dad were "winter Texans" and they would play a lot of different games during the winter months they spent in Mission, Texas. Jim is a very good bowler and I am sure he played dominos with his Grandparents while there for a bowling tournament.

"Call the guy" is Nancy's mantra. Above I alluded to the fact that "the guy" is Jim. The meaning is simple; when she is having a problem especially with computers or any technology, she calls her son James. Wouldn't it be nice if we all had a guy to call or that James lived closer to us? He fixes everything from appliances to computers to TVs.

"One chair, two pieces" has to be considered a story that could define Nancy's cleaning and organizing ability. She has always liked to have her home cleaned and organized. A place for everything; and everything in its place. She has the habit of cleaning off Dad's dining room table every time she comes to visit. He sits by that table a lot during the day for everything from eating to reading his westerns. Dad loves to read and always has a book on the table along with other important papers, pens, tissue, napkins, and those things he likes within an arm's reach. Nancy likes all that stuff out of sight. And she will put Dad's things in the corner, floor to ceiling set of cabinets. It is not unusual for Dad to call Nancy as she is making her way home to find out where she put some important item. Dad explained that she could often tell him where the missing item was placed. But let us begin the chair story.

"When you were cleaning out the garage did you find the other half of the dining room chair that was in the basement?"

was what Mom wanted to know. It was the first question she asked as Nancy and Dad returned from Stanley. Mom and Dad had lived there for less than a year because of Dad's job. They did not sell their home on Pelsdorf Road; they just rented in Stanley because it was not going to be a permanent change. Mom and Dad were moving back to Loyal. Mom had left Stanley with her last load, earlier in the day to get home and unpack the car. Dad & Nancy were going to follow; packing up everything else and making their last trip back to Loyal. Dad had a fire going and when he found half of a chair in the garage he saw no reason to keep it. Gone. When Nancy came up from the basement with the other half of the now burned chair there was no reason to keep it because the first half was already gone. If you wonder why half of the chair was in the basement and the other half was in the garage; I have no answer for you. The deal was Nancy and Dad made a pack not to say anything about the chair. Their plan would have worked if it hadn't been for Mom's memory. Nancy let Dad know she would follow his lead. This is where the story breaks down, I didn't find it or I lost it just wasn't an acceptable answer. I don't know what Mom really knew. How do they say it? Things happen!

Another family story deals with Nancy and Patricia. Once when they were visiting Dad, they found they couldn't get his TV to work for them. He was visiting Diane so they called him at her place. After trying to explain how the remote worked without much luck he asked if they could see the big red button. "Hit that and go to bed," was the solution he offered. See our Dad has a good sense of humor; it isn't like he wasn't trying to be helpful, he just couldn't explain the TV to them. It would be nice to go back to those first TVs with an on-off switch and a channel selector. I would even be willing to give up the remote and get up if I wanted a different channel. I know, those days are gone and I just have to deal with it.

As I had written earlier, Nancy lives only 20 minutes from the Mall of America. She doesn't care to go unless one of the sisters are in town and insist we go to the mall, locals aren't real big on the place but I love it. The Mall has 520 stores and 50 restaurants. No, I have not ever been in all those stores; how would that be possible? It is a different shopping experience and if I lived close I am sure I would agree with Nancy. But don't forget there is no sales tax on clothing or shoes. This last summer while my Grandkids were visiting from Tennessee we checked out the Lego store. There were 8 larger-than-life models including a Lego robot that is 34 feet tall. Andrew asked one of the guys how long it took them to make the robot. Several people working for months and he also explained that if Andrew or Parker wanted to make a display, the Lego Company would supply the pieces. Andrew's future plans are to be an author so he won't be building the next model for the store. Parker isn't sure he would be interested either. On Mother's day it has become a tradition of mine to do a 5-K with my daughter and Nancy at the Mall of America. It is a Susan B Kolmen event that gives us an opportunity to raise money for the fight against breast cancer. Our maternal Grandmother had a breast removed so all of us get our regular check-ups and keep up on the latest information because cancer struck so close to us. It is a nice Mother's Day tradition.

Nancy called me one Sunday evening as I was driving home from visiting my Grandchildren at their other Grandma's home in Schawno. She asked me the name of my favorite

TV show. I was thinking she asking about my favorite all time show. I was thinking Cheers, Seinfeld, Mash but it depends on my current mood. No, no; she wanted me to decide between The Mentalist or Person of Interest. At the time she and Pat were visiting Wisconsin while staying at Dad's. Because it was a Sunday evening I was missing The Mentalist and when it had come on as they were watching it, Nancy told Pat that this was my favorite show. Pat disagreed. She was sure Person of Interest would be my choice. I know what the confusion was all about because when I was visiting Nancy I used her treadmill to watch an episode of The Mentalist. I have all five seasons of that series and usually walk on my treadmill while watching a show on DVD. If you don't have to watch the commercials you can get it done in less than 45 minutes. Another time when Pat was visiting I had let her use my first season of Person of Interest because she was asking me about the series and what was happening. I told her she could use my copy to catch up because she didn't start watching that show when it started on TV. She had tried to pick up about half way through the second season, which means there was background information that she had missed. "Long story short" I said The Mentalist was my favorite but the answer could be Person of Interest on a Tuesday night. This meant Nancy won; sorry Pat.

Nancy's license plate bracket says, "I own a piece of the Pack" across the top and "Packer Owner" across the bottom. The story behind that bracket is she actually has one share of the Green Bay Packers, which her sisters purchased for her birthday in 2011. The cost of that one share was more than we usually spend so we decided that would be her birthday gift for a few years. According to Pam's calculations we have to buy her a gift on September 11, 2014. That date brings us to another story, where were you on 9-11-01? We were quizzing my brother JR about when his family had birthdays. He did pretty well with most of the dates but couldn't come up with all the sibling's birthdays. When he said that Nancy was born on September 11th, Zachary just laughed and asked, "How appropriate is that?" JR said we should not pick on Nancy when she isn't with us. I was pleased that JR defended Nancy since he spent a few years getting her into trouble.

Nancy is a true-blue American. I'm not sure why we don't call her a true red, white, & blue American. Where does that phrase "true-blue" come from? Google it! Nancy is the reason all four sisters have a red, white, & blue pie plate with a cake pan to match. I think it was a Christmas gift about 3 years ago. She'll decorate her home for every holiday and the 4th of July is one of the important days for her to celebrate. The first neighborhood she lived in when moving to Minneapolis had a contest for the best-decorated house on the block during the Christmas season. She would start for Halloween then just remove the scary stuff and keep adding until the day the houses were to be judged. Her neighbors never had a chance; the Locknane family usually took first. Now that Nancy has moved to another neighborhood maybe there is a chance for others to win the first-place plaque.

Once when Pat and Nancy were talking on the phone Nancy said, "It has been raining for the last three days. We are waiting for some sunshine." Pat said, "Life isn't about waiting for the storm to pass but learning how to dance in the rain." Where did you come up with that stuff?" Nancy wanted to know. (There might have been a different explicative used.)

"Read it off the planter you gave us for Christmas last year," was Patricia's reply. Oh really!

The one last story I have to share about Nancy is who does her writing. Remember when I told you she got Dad's cake for his birthday in 2012? The cake had "Isn't it heaven to be 87?" It was her husband, Jerry who is the genius behind the writing. "Isn't it great to be 88?" was my suggestion for 2013. I lost; you'll have to check out the recipes in Chapter 10 and see what they came up with for Dad's birthday cake in 2014.

8/The Pumpkin

Mom took this picture of Al's children in 2007. The location was Foxfire Gardens in Marshfield, Wisconsin. Left to right: Mikayla 8, Trevor 11, Nikki 13.

Albert is 5 years younger than Nancy, making him the baby in the family when born in 1962. One thing about being the baby when you are born is that you are always the baby even when you reach 50 years of age. Is being the baby good or bad? I can't say; we'll have to check with brother Al. Dad likes the story of Albert and his ice. Al rode with Dad on the milk route and once he decided to collect some ice that was on the floor of the factory. Dad carried ice in a chest where he stored milk samples. When he got to the factory he would dump the old ice and get new for the next load. The ice Al collected he stored in his pockets. Little boys like to collect things to carry in their pockets. The big wet spot on Al's pants was Dad's first clue that the little guy was collecting ice. Dad was going to try to get him to dump the ice but it was almost gone and the pants were already wet. Now Albert collects other things; keep reading.

Years ago when Mom would call us to eat supper and we were watching TV I'm not sure what was so very interesting but when we didn't get to the table ASAP, the TV would go black. Al would have been just a little guy because this would happen in Maple Park. I don't know that I ever figured it out until Mom told me. When we were called and didn't arrive at the supper table, my parents wouldn't call us again. Dad would go to the basement and turn the fuse out. TV would go black and we would head to the kitchen to eat. I think it is said parents should pick their battles. Guess that was one of those battles our parents felt they didn't need to fight.

Another time when Al was just a little guy something happened to make him cry. I tried to comfort him but he wasn't going to settle for my comfort. Then I thought about giving him something to drink; you can't drink and cry at the same time. It worked and I learned something I would use years later when I was teaching. I had a kindergarten student in my Physical Education that was really crying up a storm. This is upsetting to all the other students so I offered him the opportunity to get a drink; again it worked.

I used this trick for the 12 years I taught at the elementary level. Only one student ever questioned my idea. Once when a student came to me crying about hurting his arm I told he to get a drink, another little boy asked, "How will that help his arm?" I told the second little boy we should just watch the first little guy as he went to the water fountain; yes it worked because it is hard to drink and cry. Kids; you got to love them.

During the years when I was in college whenever I called home someone was there to answer the phone. Mom didn't work outside the home and I knew when she was taking my siblings to school so didn't call at those times. Once, no one answered when I called and I had to call back a few times before Mom finally did answer. I told her I had been worried about them because no one answered the phone. She just laughed because I was so naive. Another time Albert answered the phone and I asked what he was doing. "Scissoring for Dad" was his reply. Later Dad explained they were tying some quilts for Mom. Tying quilts could be a big family project. The quilting frame had to be set up using the backs of four chairs, one at each corner. The frame consisted of four long boards covered with some material held together with clips. The material allows for pins to be used to hold the quilt in place. First the bottom of the quilt is pinned in place, then the batting, and then the top of the quilt. The tying is done with yarn. The needle is sent from the top to the bottom and back to the top to be tied. Albert got to cut the yarn when Dad was finished with each stitch or tie. Because of the time and space it took to up usually Mom had two or three quilt tops ready to be tied. It was a good deal to have the help of that 5-year old. Actually, I know it demonstrates the level of patience our parents had with all of us.

Our Dad would play Santa for us. Mom had a Santa suit with a full mask so the only thing we ever noticed was that just about the time Dad would go outside to look for Santa, the jolly red guy would come. As Pat and I got older we would play Santa for the younger kids. Once Albert made the observation that Santa had small hands. That was the time Patricia was Santa and it could have been the last time we had the real Santa handout gifts.

There was an Oleson family that lived about 4 miles from us in Maple Park, they had an in-ground swimming pool. We were invited to swim anytime we were interested if they were home. Swimming at Oleson's was one thing that Albert remembers about living in Illinois. He and Florence Oleson; the mother of the family, were very good friends. We left Illinois after Al had finished kindergarten so he was really young. I'm not sure he remembers swimming at midnight but some people do. Apparently after midnight suits were optional. There was even a time that Dad went off the board into the deep end. Now Dad could not swim; but he was wearing an inner tube. We don't want this book to be X-rated so I think we'll stop with the after midnight swimming parties but it is common knowledge that over the years stories get embellished each time they are retold.

When I asked my brothers and sisters what they remember about Grandpa and Grandma Eder's tavern the younger ones all mentioned the warm cashews that were behind the bar. There was a unit that sat on the back bar which kept various kinds of nuts warm and ready to serve. Al says he can remember getting some warm cashews for the ride home but they were usually gone just about the time our car pulled out of the driveway. That driveway wasn't much longer than crossing a ditch; there was no length to it at all. Patricia remembers sitting at the bar and drinking ginger ale; which she felt looked like beer. Her thought was, "hey look at me." Kids! But then I recall drinking Squirt. It was only a 6-ounce bottle with a little guy pictured on the side of the bottle. My two older cousins, Tom and Bob would have a contest to see who could drink down the fastest to save the little guy. When I joined their contest I never won; I couldn't drink that carbonated stuff fast enough. Another thing we all remember was that Grandpa Eder would give us silver dollars for Christmas or our birthdays. Patricia said she put her money in her savings account at the bank in Maple Park. Pat was very disappointed when she took her money out because she was expecting to get those silver dollars back and not the paper money or check she received. Interesting what kids remember and think about their adult world, isn't?

As I have written before Mom and Dad were very protective of us. Before Al was born, there was a child, Maria Ridulp kidnapped off a Sycamore street corner in December of 1957. At the time of the kidnapping, Nancy was only a baby and our sister Patty was 7 years old, the age of the child taken. We lived about 15 miles from Sycamore and were never allowed to wander the streets even when we were visiting our cousins who lived in that town. When I was growing up I didn't understand what all the fuss was about if Mom couldn't see us at all times; now with children and grandchildren of my own I have a clearer understanding. On September 14, 2012 (which was my parent's 66th wedding anniversary) Jack McCullough was convicted of the kidnapping and killing of this young child 55 years earlier. A photograph of her sitting on her mother's lap in front of a Christmas tree appeared in the paper. When I saw that picture in 2012 I did a double take because the girl looked like an old picture of me. Our hair was dark and both of us had the same hairstyle. The reason McCullough was finally caught was because his mother had given him an alibi in 1957 when he was picked up for questioning. In 1994, while on her deathbed, she confessed to her daughter about the coverup. She didn't want to take that lie to her grave. Think of how all those families were affected by this event. I write about this now because it does explain part of the reason why my parents were so protective. This level of protection was raised to another level when Albert was born. It is best if I just say, this last one might have been Mom's favorite; but who could blame her, he was a cute little guy.

In 1968 when we moved to Wisconsin Al had just finished kindergarten; which means he never went to St. Peter & Paul school like the rest of us. We all attended public school for kindergarten, so Al went to Maple Park for that one year of kindergarten. The building where he attended school that year was the high school that our mother attended years earlier. Another family that lived only about a mile from us in the same direction as the Olesons was the Thur family. Again; Mrs. Thur always enjoyed our little brother. One day Mrs. Thur called Mom and asked if we were missing Al? We didn't know, but yes, guess he wasn't with us. He had gotten on his tricycle and peddled his way to her home or he might have been going to swim at Olseon's. Who was supposed to be watching that kid? Guess I was, but the Lord took care of him. The county road we lived on proved to be very busy at certain times of the day. Mom thanked her Lord more than once that Al got out of our sight during one of the less busy times. He had gone about a mile on that little bike.

Our first year in Wisconsin, Albert remembers Mom helping him with a Halloween costume in first grade. He thinks it was her idea to dress him in all black and take corn stalks to tie on his body. He was a little corn stalk and he took first place in his class contest. He even had his picture printed in the Loyal paper. Here was this little guy from Illinois beating all the locals for first place. Now, 50 years later he and his family are the locals, but they aren't getting beat. When his kids attended school in Marshfield we would always have to check the pictures of students in the paper because I believe all three, at different times were in the paper for something they had done at school. I know Trevor was in the Marshfield News Herald more than once. Photographers look for a cute kid because they make for great pictures. If that cute kid won the spelling bee, it was even better.

Up to this point I have not addressed the issue of Mom's habit of saving. When she was a child there was a war effort to save things for the soldiers on the front line. She explained to me once that they were taught to use what you have or save it for another day. She found it hard to toss things or get rid of them. Remembering the chair story, she did know where most things were and she could find stuff. Mom was not even close to any of those hoarders you see on TV. Once I told Pat that Mom was always trying to give me stuff I didn't want. "Take it," Pat told me. "Then you can get rid of it." She made a very good point, which became our strategy to help Mom downsize. If one of her children picked up on the idea of collecting and saving I would have to say it is Albert. Many people have collections. Mom collected yarn and sewing or quilting material. After her death when we cleared away her things it was amazing how much yarn she had collected. When she crotched a project she always wanted to start with enough yarn to complete the project because if she had to purchase more of a color it might be a different shade when not purchased at the same time. Because she always purchased extra she had some left over from every thing she made. In her things we found a note or article she saved, which was titled "Stuff." It explained how we try every fall to sort our stuff into good and bad piles. When we die our children will want the good stuff and the bad stuff will go to the dump. It goes on to say that it doesn't matter what happens to our stuff after we die because we still have the good stuff God has prepared for us in heaven. There was no author listed but it was a nice thought. We all collect things that we like, enjoy, or have inherited. So Albert collects safes. None of my reasons explain why my brother collects them. Yes, those big huge heavy items available after a bank or jewelry store closes; the safe. He started with coins and then needed a place to keep them so that would explain the first one. His collection of safes did get up to 35 or more of various sizes but now he is selling some of them when he can find the right buyer. When he remodeled the place where his family lives now; he built one into the basement of the house. That won't be going anywhere anytime soon. Actually the place that Mom and Dad lived on Pelsdorf Road was the first place that Al had a built-in a safe. In the raised basement of that home there was a sliding door that allowed for the larger safe to be moved into their home. Al said he just built a wall around it and that safe won't ever get moved. It was sold with the house when our parents moved to town.

When I asked Al how he came up with the idea of collecting safes he said, "Because they are inexpensive and no one wants to move them. Let me tell you about hauling a safe. Dad & I could get one for free from a fire station in Illinois.

So I drove my ½ ton Ford 150 short bed to Illinois to pick it up. At the same time I was going to get a couch from my cousin, Greg Eder. The couch was for my son, Kevin who was in college at the time. We had really big plans for that little truck. The safe was going to be loaded first because we didn't figure it could be moved after it was on the truck. When they used the end loader to put it on my truck it almost picked the front wheels off the ground. "Take it off, take it off," was my cry. We had to take it off and leave it for another day, only the couch made it back to Wisconsin that weekend. Dad took his ¾ ton truck that he used to pull their motor home to Texas and picked up the safe. Because Dad drove down to Illinois and back in one day Kevin rode with him so he could help with the driving. When Dad dropped my son off at home Dad told Kevin to tell me to get a "real truck." I liked my ½ ton because it got better gas mileage but I didn't ever try to haul a safe around again. Al is right; people don't like to move those safes. Another thing Al has is Grandpa Eder's slot machine. To start a collection of slot machines would cost lots of money and storage becomes the issue. He has passed the collecting bug on to his son Trevor, who collects cigar boxes. Now there is something I would be willing to haul.

Al graduated from Loyal High School in 1980 and went into construction work. He isn't with the same company but still enjoys working in the building industry. Thus the reason he has been able to build his safes into where ever he is living. He and his ex-wife, Rhonda remain friends and had three children before their divorce. All three of the children live with Al in a country home that is near the Marshfield Speedway. All three of his children have worked at the speedway while in high school. It made a great part-time job for Nikki and Trevor. Mikayka, the youngest is a freshman at Marshfield high school. She is currently working at the speedway for extra speeding money. Nikki graduated from senior high in 2012 and is pursuing a career in nursing. She is considering joining the Reserves to get some help with her education. Trevor is a senior this year and plans to study to be a mechanic after he graduates. Trevor has always looked just like his father; that is to say when Al was younger. Trevor was pictured in the paper more than once. Like I wrote before, those photographers always look for the cute kids. Yes, and once it wasn't that he was just cute, he had taken first in a spelling bee.

Al took his three kids to the Mall of America to see the Nicelodeon Universe, which is the world's largest indoor theme park. There is also Sea Life Aquarium, which has hands-on activities for students to learn about life under water. The 300-foot Ocean Tunnel is not for anyone that is claustrophobia but it gives you an opportunity to see what it would be like under the ocean. Nancy went with on this family outing because we all know how much she loves that big mall. But really Al; no shopping? There are almost 500 stores in that Mall. That might have been the first time Mom would have been disappointed in Albert. Mom was a "shop 'till you drop kind of gal." But then Nancy said Al's kids did really enjoy their time at the Mall.

Because we all have the same parents we do look alike to a point. Each of the six of us has our own personality and temperament but on the phone it is difficult to be sure who is on the other end. Every Friday night, for almost the past two years my family and I have been taking Dad out for a fish fry on Friday night. We like to go to the American Legion in

Loyal because the bartender, Carol has our drinks ready and on the bar if she sees us walk in the door. Raymond's brandy old-fashion is always the first drink on the bar followed by Dad's wine cooler; why would those guys want to go anywhere else? So when I arrive to pick Dad up it isn't unusual for him to tell me to call Pam. One Friday night he picked up the phone to dial the number for me and handed me the phone. When Pam answered I asked how she was doing and when the reply was, "good, now that I am finished typing my transcript" I was confused. Before my thought of "when did Pam start-typing transcripts" was complete; I realized I was talking to Patricia. I should have realized something was up when Dad handed me the phone because of his strange grin. I wanted to relate this story to you because maybe it will make the next story more believable. A few years ago I was in Fleet picking up something for the farm and I saw my brother Ralph. The stocking cap should have been my clue but I find it so easy to ignore clues. After talking to him for just a few minutes I realized it was Albert in front of me. Ralph never wears stocking hats and there was a reason he seemed to be a little shorter. Those two brothers of mine do look and sound very similar if you aren't paying close attention or if you are in a hurry. Those are the only excuses I have for my mistake.

One family story that Mom would add would be the cheese story. At Kevin and Sarah's wedding Mom had a piece of cheese on her plate that she was waiting to eat. She wanted it to be at room temperature. Her father always said that was the best way to eat cheese was at room temperature not right out of the refrigerator. Albert and his family came for the dance and not the supper. He must have been hungry because when he saw that piece of cheese he just popped it in his mouth. Grandpa was right but Mom explained that she was planning to eat that piece of cheese in a few minutes. Cute only goes so far.

Another thing I should say about both of my brothers is that they are wonderful in their roles as fathers. Yes, they did have a great example to follow because Dad was always good to his children. Our Mother was always good to us and the four girls all turned out to be good mothers to their offspring. It must be my double standard that I live with that I didn't find the need to relate that fact until I got to the boys. Women are expected to be good mothers in my world and if they are smart, they select men to marry that make good fathers. In my world lots of things are black and white; shades of gray can complicate a person's life. One last note: I love my brothers; they are simply amazing. I just couldn't imagine my life without them.

9/A Picture Is Worth A Thousand Words

It was really hard to select only 25 pictures for this book. I wanted one from each of the six families formed by Mom & Dad's children. It was easier to have two pictures from Pam's family; one of her immediate family and one of just her grandchildren. Because I used 9 pictures earlier in the book I have the 16 remaining ones in this chapter. Coming up with the correct dates for these pictures was difficult. It made for an evening of family fun in September of 2013 getting everyone to voice their opinion. Again, not sure who is right but we came up with a collective story and we don't plan to change it. Enjoy.

What was the occasion for this picture? Dad wasn't sure but he got dressed up so they took his picture. It might have been his Confirmation about 1940.

Mom graduated from Maple Park High School in 1945. She was a classmate of Dad's sister Esther.

Here is Dad with his mother in front of the family farm I remember. Dad thinks it was Mother's Day in 1946. He and Mom were married that September. The reason we came up with the year was because Dad is sure he was not married when this picture was taken.

On the back of the original of this picture, Mom wrote; "Ed Schmal took the picture on his farm when Chuck Snyder's cattle were in the corn." In was taken about 1962 and I remember helping Dad spot the cattle from the plane. When we saw some of the cattle we had to land to tell the others where to find them. A cell phone would have been helpful. Dad is the third person from the left. This was his Cessna 170A. He sold it when we moved to Wisconsin.

The occasion was Mom and Dad's 17th anniversary. Front row left to right; Ralph JR, 7 Dad holding Albert, 18 months Nancy, 6 and Mom. Back row; Pam, 10 Patricia, 13 and Connie, 15. We are sure of this information because again Mom took the time to write on the back of the picture.

This picture was taken when Dad purchased his first diesel in 1961. The picture was used as an advertisement. The salesman explained to Dad that he had to be paid. Dad received one dollar.

This picture is of poor quality but it has to be used. Grandpa and Grandma are celebrating their 50th wedding anniversary with all of their children. From left to right; Louie, Bob, Sis, Jean, Grandpa John, Esther, Grandma Margaret, Betty, Loretta, Ralph (my Dad), Fran, Katherine, and John. Uncle John is almost out of the picture but we know he is good looking.

This picture was taken in 1975 at Ralph JR's wedding. We are at the American Legion in Loyal. Pictured in front are Mom and Dad. Back row from left to right: Nancy, Albert, Pam, Connie, JR, Patricia.

This picture was taken at a Schmitt family reunion in 1977. Grandpa had been gone for five years. Back row left to right; Fran, Louie, Loretta, Grandma, Jean, Bob, Kay. Front row; Sis, Esther, Ralph (my Dad), and John. Missing is Betty.

The year is 1986 and the occasion is my parents' 40th wedding anniversary. This is Mom's family. From left to right; Eleanor, Mom, Dad, Anton (Bud), Barb (She is Bud's wife) and Helen.

This was taken for the church directory at St Anthony's in Loyal. We did all dress up nice that day to celebrate Mom and Dad's 40 years together.

December 1998: Mom and Dad had started to go to Texas during the winter months. Thus we don't have them in this picture. After this year we started to celebrate Christmas in July or August because then our parents could celebrate with us. In a perfect world we would be able to see both of Al's eyes.

This is Easter 1999 at Pam's home. Ralph's head didn't make it into the original so I just couldn't do anything about it here. I gave Nancy her "Friends don't let friends be Viking fans" shirt.

This was taken for my parents' 55th wedding anniversary. We celebrated at the Legion in Loyal and the year was 2001. I don't think all six of us were at the event at the same time is the reason we don't have a family picture. Patricia did try to get into the frame.

This is our Christmas celebration in September 2001. Like all family pictures there had to be a few taken to get a good picture of all eight of us. Patricia's eyes might be closed on this one but there was another one where Nancy had bunny ears. We had Albert hug his two sisters so we could have a photo without extra ears.

Mom could not talk for the last year of her life. She had been battling cancer for almost 10 years. This is one of the last wonderful pictures we have of Mom. It was taken on May 5th, 2007 on her 80th birthday. We didn't get to celebrate 81 years with her but this last birthday was wonderful. Mom is holding a stepping stone from Valerie. It says, "if Grandparents were flowers I'd pick you first."

10/ Cast of Characters and a few family recipes

Here is our family tree.

Dad's paternal Grandparents:

Louis Schmitt B 9-18-1863 + Katherine Mittman B 10-23-1863

Their children: Mary Schmitt B 1889, John Schmitt (Dad's father) B 1891 D 3-4-1972, Albert Schmitt B 1892, Louis Schmitt Jr B 1894.

Dad's maternal Grandparents:

Gustav Loerzel B 11-22-1895 + Katherine Weirhus B 9-22-1863

Their children: Anna Loerzel B 7-22-1892 D 11-22-1944, Joseph Loerzel B 3-14-1896 D 8-28-1971, Margaret Loerzel (Dad's mother) B 5-10-1894 D 12-8-1978, Rose Loerzel B 8-22-1897 D 12-14-1980.

Dad's parents:

John Schmitt B 1891 +10-7-1913 Margaret Loerzel B 5-10-1894

Their children and Grandchildren:

Katherine M Schmitt (1915) + Raymond B McDonald (1913) Grandchildren; Phyllis Irene (1936), Margaret H (1937), Jerald G (1939), Raymond Paul (1942), Sylvia J (1951), Elizabeth R Schmitt (1918) + John Sauber (1907),

Grandchildren; John J (1937), Donald G (1938), Sandra L (1949), Betsy A (1952)

Frances M Schmitt (1920) + George Altepeter (1901)

Grandchildren; Loretta M (1938), Helen M (1940), Ruth A (1944), Linda J (1951), Victoria A (1954), Anita M (1958)

Loretta A Schmitt (1922) + Matthias Schramer

Grandchildren; Mary Louise (1941), Dorothy M (1942), Jane I (1946), Susan H (1949), Lorraine A (1951), James J (1957), Michael J (1961)

Louis C Schmitt (1924) + Clara Schramer

Grandchildren; Larry C (1948), Gary J (1950), Diane M (1952), Janet L (1953), Dennis A (1955), John B (1956), Edward J (1957), Catherine A (1960), Thomas P (1962), Leslie D (1964), Robert P (1965), Teresa E (1967), Andrew L (1968)

Ralph F Schmitt*Dad (1925) + Mary M Eder*Mom (1927)

Their children, G=Grandchildren and GG=Great-Grandchildren:

Constance M (1948) + Raymond C Milz (1947)

G: Valerie L (1972) + Mark Provost

G: Kevin Ray (1977) + Sarah J Michel

GG: Carson W (2005), Andrew M (2006), Parker T (2008)

Patricia L (1950) + John J Sauber (1950)

G: Lisa M (1971) + David Welch

GG: Braydon M (1999) GG: Josilyn S (2001)

G: Stephanie L (1974) + Shawn Snell (1975)

GG: Quentin C (2011)

G: Kimberly A (1977) + Scott Karr (1970)

GG: Nathan D (2005)

Pamela A (1953) + Randy Meyer (1953)

G: Jennifer (1972) + Chad Bogdonvich (1973)

GG: Kaylee (1997), Tragen (2000), Amanda (2002)

G: Peggy S (1974 + Paul Miller (1964)

GG: Kyle (1997)

G: Jodi (1976)

GG: Addison J (2013)

G: John Meyer (1979) + Maria (1980)

GG: Alexis M (2007) GG: Jackson J (2008); G: Kurt (1981) + Lori (1982) GG: Brittney A (2005) GG: Sidney A (2006) GG: Gage A (2008) GG: Kolt (2009) GG: Wyatt A (2011) GG: Kortney (2012); G: Kris (1983) GG: Ty (2004)

Ralph JR. (1956) + Shelby

G: Zachary + Amy

GG: Hunter GG: Katie

Nancy J (1957) + Jerry Locknane (1941)

G: Christy (1975) + Jason Smith (1972)

GG: Ryan (2001) GG: Austin (2002)

G: James (1981)

Albert J (1962) + Rhonda

G: Nikki (1994); G: Treavor (1996); G: Mikayla (1998)

Esther M Schmitt + Howard Warber

Grandchildren; Donna M (1948), Dennis C (1950), Dale E (1954), Dean A (1957)

Nicholas Schmitt (1929) Twin to Margaret

Margaret M Schmitt + Bernard Brewsey (1921)

Grandchildren; Ronald (1947), Steven (1949), James (1950), Bernadette (1951), Timothy (1958), Michael (1964), Thomas (1965)

Jean M Schmitt (1931) + George Ramer (1931)

Grandchildren; Karen M (1951), David (1965), Patricia S (1966)

John L Schmitt (1933) + Diana M Ganoe

Grandchildren; Debbra M (1956), Wilburn D (1960), Roger J (1962), Joan M (1965)

Robert J Schmitt (1935) + Janice L Lorenz (1938)

Grandchildren; Duane R (1955), Gail D (1956), Lynette (1960), Ann M (1971)

Mom's maternal Great-Great-Grandparents:
Philip and Elizabeth Walchshofer
Mom's maternal Great-Grandparents:
Joseph and Elizabeth (Walchshofer) Bircheneder
Mom's maternal Grandparents:
Joseph and Katherine (Kreipl) Bircheneder
Mom's paternal Grandparents
Josef and Maria Eder
Mom's parents:
Anton Eder and Helen Bircheneder
Their children and G=Grandchildren
Helen Eder + Bud Studebaker; G: Thomas, Robert, Kathy, Richard, and Chris
Mary Margaret (Mom) + Ralph F Schmitt Note: our family is listed above.
Eleanor + Jerome Stowe; G: Chuck, Roger, and Daniel
Anton (Bud) Eder + Barb Reynolds; G: Greg, Gwen, and Karen

While families love their stories; they also have recipes that they love. I asked each of my siblings to give me a recipe that they remember from our younger days. What do they remember and maybe even miss from when we were growing up together? Here is the result with a note about why it was selected. Keep in mind; my mother was a great cook. She always enjoyed Mr. Food, a chef that was on TV. Art Ginsburg(1931-2012) was Mr. Food with the registered trade mark "Ooh. It's so good!" That is what he would say after presenting a new recipe on TV. Mom met him and had her picture taken with him. He always had things that were quick, easy and practical. I don't know that we have any of his ideas here, but just google him and you'll find plenty.

<u>Constance Mary</u>: The reason I wanted to put this recipe in was because Mom loved potato salad. If we were going to have a picnic, we were going to have potato salad. Mom always said that potato salad was better on the second day if it was kept cool in the refrigerator. I don't know that this was Mom's favorite potato salad recipe because she did enjoy trying different ones. She did tell me a good mayonnaise and yellow mustard were the two ingredients that were a must.

<u>Potato Salad</u>
Ingredients:
4 eggs
1 ½ pounds of potatoes; halved & quartered
Salt & pepper
1-cup mayonnaise
¼ cup buttermilk
1 onion, peeled
2 stalks of celery, chopped
1-teaspoon paprika
2 teaspoons finely chopped parsley
3 tablespoons vinegar
2 tablespoons yellow mustard
1 tablespoon Worcestershire

Directions:
Put the eggs in a medium pot and cover with water. Bring to a full boil then cover and turn off the heat. Let the eggs stand for 10 minutes. Put in cold water to cool. Put potatoes in a large pot covered with salted water. Bring to boil and cook until tender; takes 12 to 15 minutes over medium heat. Drain. Grate the onion over the potatoes. After cooled stir in celery, paprika, parsley. Add salt & pepper to taste. In a small bowl, combine buttermilk, mayonnaise, vinegar,

mustard, and Worcestershire as dressing. Add eggs to the potatoes and pour in dressing. Mix to cover eggs and potatoes with the dressing.

Patricia Lee: added this recipe to our book because Mom gave it to her and now it is served daily at JJ Jamokes in Caro, MI. JJ Jamokes is owned and operated by John Sauber. On their web site: http://www.jjjamokes.com it says they use a variety of Michigan beans to make the stew a favorite of customers. Pat says that this stew can also be made in a crock-pot.

Harlequin Bean Stew
Ingredients:
1 can red kidney beans (drained)
1 can lima beans (drained)
1 can butter beans (drained)
1 can pork & beans
2 large onions
½ pound of bacon
¼ teaspoon dry mustard
1-cup brown sugar
½ cup vinegar

Directions:
Brown onions and bacon. Simmer dry mustard, brown sugar and vinegar in a small saucepan for 10 minutes. Add all to bean mixture. Bake at 350 degrees.

Pamela Ann: She remembers making this with Mom during the holiday season. It didn't always turn out the same but the results were always delicious or should I say divine? This was a family favorite. As you read the directions it becomes clear that everything has to be ready and it helps to have two people working to get it right.

Divinity
Ingredients:
4 cups sugar
1-cup light corn syrup
¾ cup water
3 egg whites stiffly beaten
1-teaspoon vanilla
1 cup broken nuts

Directions:
Place sugar, syrup, & water in a saucepan over low heat. Stir until sugar is dissolved. Then allow mixture to cook without stirring. The temperature needs to get to 255 degrees. To test; a little drop in cold water forms a ball. Remove from heat and pour beating constantly in a fine stream into the egg whites. Continue beating until the mixture holds its shape and loses its gloss. Add the vanilla and nuts. Now drop quickly from the tip of a spoon onto waxed paper in individual peaks. Or mixture can be spread in a buttered pan to be cut into 1-inch squares when the mixture is firm.

Ralph Frank JR: OK, it isn't like Ralph gave me this recipe. He never did get a recent picture to me so I didn't even ask him to think about food. He is a busy guy; working, riding the Harley, and visiting friends. I know he likes to eat healthy (or at least he should) so I came up with one of the ways he would eat an apple.

<u>Snickers Salad</u>
Ingredients:
6-8 granny Smith apples
6 regular size snickers bars
8 ounces of sour cream
16 ounces of cool whip

Directions:
Peel and cut up apples into bite-size pieces. Cut up snicker bars small pieces. Mix all the ingredients together. Enjoy.

<u>Nancy Josephine</u>: Nancy says this is a recipe that Mom gave her. Her husband, Jerry often makes up the batter while Nancy is at work. Isn't he a great guy to keep around? Nance says it makes lots, thus the name.

<u>Monster Bars</u>
Ingredients:
½ cup butter
1-cup white sugar
1-cup brown sugar
3 eggs
1 ½ cup peanut butter
1-teaspoon vanilla
2 teaspoons baking soda
4-½ cups oatmeal
1-½ cups chocolate ships
1-½ cups M-Ms

Directions:
Cream the butter and add sugars. Add eggs, peanut butter and mix. Stir in vanilla, baking soda, and oatmeal. Once all

is mixed add the chips and M-Ms. Grease a 10 X 15 pan. Bake at 350 degrees for 25 minutes.

Albert James: Again, I didn't get input from Al but I can remember Mom making this cake many times. Because of the candy bars it is a very moist cake and everyone loves it. I don't even want to think about the calories. You don't need the frosting; the cake is great with a little ice cream.

Milky Way Cake
Ingredients:
8 Milky Way candy bars
2 sticks of butter
2 cups sugar
4 eggs
2-¼ cups flour
½ teaspoon salt
½ teaspoon baking soda
1-cup buttermilk (+1 Tablespoon)
2 teaspoons vanilla
1-2 cups powdered sugar

Directions:
Melt 5 candy bars (3 are for the frosting, not to eat) with 1 stick of butter over low heat. Cream sugar and eggs and beat well. Add the flour, salt, baking soda, and buttermilk. When well mixed add the candy mixture and vanilla. When well blended, pour into 9 X 13 greased pan. Bake at 300 degrees for one hour. Frost when cooled. To make frosting, melt a stick of butter with 3 Milky Way bars. Then add a tablespoon of buttermilk and a teaspoon of vanilla with enough powdered sugar to stiffen. Frost while in the pan.

Grandpa's Cookies These are favorites of all the Dad's grandchildren. If Dad is coming to your home for a visit or for the holidays these are the cookies he will bring. Yes, he makes them himself. The sisters have gotten together to do a cookie exchange and he always likes to join us. He does not vary from his cookie selection.

Ingredients:

Ritz crackers

Peanut Butter

Melting chocolate

Directions:

Using a double boiler, melt the chocolate. Put peanut butter between two crackers. Dip the two crackers into the chocolate and place on wax paper to cool and dry. The cookies can be stacked after the chocolate has set.

Better Than Sex Chocolate Cake This was the cake for Dad's 88th birthday celebration.

Ingredients:

18 1/2 ounce package German chocolate cake mix

14 ounce can sweetened condensed milk

21 ounce jar of butterscotch caramel fudge topping

12 ounce carton of frozen whipped topping thawed

3 Heath candy bars, crushed

Directions:

Heat the oven to 350 degrees. Grease and flour 9 X 13 X 2 inch pan. Prepare and bake the cake as directed on package. When cake is still warm, but not hot, poke holes in the cake about one inch apart. You can use the handle of a wooden spoon. Pour sweetened condensed milk over the cake, and then pour the caramel fudge over the cake. Refrigerate until completely cooled which takes about an hour. Top with the whipped topping and the crushed candy bars. Keep in the refrigerator. Won't last long and don't even ask about the calories.

<u>One More for a Sore Throat</u> If you wake up with a sore throat drink this and you'll be better in one hour.
Ingredients:
2 Tablespoons of honey
2 Tablespoons of vinegar
2 Tablespoons of lemon juice
1 dash of cinnamon

Directions:
Add all four of the above ingredients in a cup of warm water and drink. If you don't feel better in an hour then it is out of my control, you'll have to call a doctor unless you can just endure and it goes away in two to three days.

It is my wish that you have enjoyed this collection of family stories and recipes. Keep in mind that "life is a journey, not a destination." I am no longer sure where I first heard that but it did make me think about my approach to life. I mention this because while my book has come to an end, it is by no means complete. Every time our family gets together there are new chapters to consider and more stories remembered. Because "the Lord has done great things for me, I am filled with joy" (Psalm 126:3) and I am thankful that you have taken the time to read my book. While it is my first attempt it is not my last published work. Give me another year or two and consider looking for another book by CM Mary.

Acknowledgements

Since Mom's death our Dad has done some writing about his life. The document he has produced is what I used as a guide to record and publish the story of his life and our family. My sister Patricia took the time to type most of Dad's memoir. If Dad and Patty had not put in all that effort this book would not have been written.